Louis Napoleon and Strasbourg

Louis Napoleon in 1836

Louis Napoleon and Strasbourg

Shirley J. Black

Edited and Revised by B.D. Gooch

Ferrell Publications
Silverton, Colorado

By the same author
Napoleon III and Mexican Silver

Library of Congress Control Number: 2003114466

ISBN: 0-9676777-3-4

Table of Contents

Preface

By 1836 the surviving relatives of the fallen Emperor Napoleon had been exiled from France for over 20 years. While nearly all had passively accepted their plight, an exception was a nephew, Charles Louis Napoleon Bonaparte, a son of Napoleon's brother Louis. Generally known to history as Louis Napoleon, at Strasbourg in 1836, he vainly initiated a short-lived insurrection which he hoped would overthrow the Orleanist government of King Louis Philippe and result in a Bonaparte restoration.

The unsuccessful attempt was ridiculed by the government as a youthful, foolhardy fiasco – and as such entered virtually all accounts of this era of French history. Although Louis Napoleon finally came to power in 1848, when he was overthrown in 1870 the succeeding republicans took up the same interpretation of the 1836 events. This version continued throughout the Third Republic and, unfortunately, is still the accepted orthodoxy in most historical accounts of the 1830s.

In 1840 at Boulogne Louis Napoleon failed again to topple the July Monarchy and once more attracted the same ridicule from the government and most historians. The extreme fragility of Louis Philippe's position rarely received proper attention and alternate explanations have enjoyed little enduring acceptance. While clear misjudgments occurred in both attempts, it has generally been overlooked that neither episode was lightly undertaken and in each case the commitment of resources was substantial.

This book by Shirley J. Black is based on unpublished material as well as a broader array of published contemporary sources than any account heretofore and joins the small handful of current narratives which offer a corrective to the orthodox version of the Strasbourg affair. By the time of her death in 1996, the author had finished the bulk of her research on the subject and drafted most of the chapters. Responsibility for the note on sources and for revising, editing, and completing the manuscript has been mine; but the final work has also benefited substantially from the interest and efforts of Freda Carley Peterson, whose technical assistance and continued encouragement in my completion of the project have been essential.

Brison D. Gooch

Chapter One

The Bonaparte Heir

Late Monday evening, October 31, 1836, the French minister of war, General Simon Bernard, received an alarming telegram from General Theophile Voirol, the Strasbourg commandant. It was dated the previous day. "This morning about six o'clock Louis Napoleon, son of the Duchess of Saint Leu, who had artillery Colonel Vaudrey <u>in</u> <u>his</u> <u>confidence</u>, went throughout Strasbourg streets with a part of . . . ." There, the frustrating despatch ended.

When the telegraph director, Alphonse Foy, delivered the message, he added a further unsettling note. "We are in doubt as to the words underlined. Fog along the line does not allow us to clear up the doubtful passage or to receive the end of the despatch." Darkness was also a factor but the mention of fog struck a raw nerve. Fog! The month of fog in the revolutionary calendar was Brumaire, October 22–November 20, a reminder of Napoleon Bonaparte's coup on 18 Brumaire thirty-seven years earlier.

The minister of war hastily handed the telegram on to the interior minister, Adrien Gasparin, who immediately shared it with his mentor, the minister of public instruction, François Guizot. Anxiety increased as they grimly scrutinized the piece of paper. Particularly disquieting, the telegram was dated almost two days earlier, 8:30 Sunday morning, October 30. For over forty hours Paris was to remain unaware of any disturbance in this sensitive border garrison. News of an implied coup was startling; and delayed, incomplete information only escalated the tension. The sixty-three year old King Louis Philippe was anguished and dismayed by this apparent challenge from Napoleon's nephew and heir. He urgently summoned his ministers who rushed to the Tuileries. It was almost midnight, Monday, October 31.

This ministry, formed less than two months earlier, on September 6, 1836, had been hand picked by Louis Philippe. Most had previously served Napoleon. Fifty-five year old Count Louis Mathieu Molé, son of a victim of the guillotine, minister of finance in 1813 and one of the fallen emperor's favorites, served as president of the council and minister of foreign affairs. Elegant, extremely courteous and detached from all political parties, he had neither ardent supporters nor implacable enemies. The minister of public instruction was forty-nine year old François Guizot, by far the dominant figure in the ministry. A Protestant whose father had been executed during the Revolution, under the Empire he had risen to become professor of history at the Sorbonne. Count Adrien de Gasparin, fifty-four year old minister of the interior, controlled the civil administration and, of critical importance, the police. Regarded as merely one of Guizot's "creatures" by Louis Blanc, he had been a cavalry officer during the Empire, serving under Murat. Admiral Claude du Camp de Rosamel, sixty-two year old minister of the navy and "an outright imbecile" according to a colleague, had served Napoleon as a naval officer. Charles Tanneguy Count Duchatel, minister of finance at only thirty-three, was Napoleon's godson and had been baptized with Louis Napoleon by the emperor's uncle, Cardinal Fesch. The fifty-seven year old minister of war was General Simon Bernard, a military engineer. In disgrace after Waterloo, he served in the United States until recalled in 1830 by Louis Philippe to be his aide-de-camp. Jean Charles Persil, the fifty year old minister of justice and public worship, would later be appointed councillor-of-state and a senator of the Second Empire. Joseph Martin du Nord was minister of commerce, agriculture and public works. A forty-six year old lawyer from Douai, he had been a supporter of the Bourbon Restoration before rallying to Louis

Philippe. These were the men assembled at the Tuileries. All were alarmed.

Guizot's *Mémoires* later revealed the trepidation of that evening. After Gasparin and Guizot had studied the telegram, the two troubled ministers "immediately" went to the Tuileries. Within "a few moments" the cabinet had assembled. That Monday night, October 31, 1836, the Orleanist government clearly considered itself threatened by Louis Napoleon Bonaparte.

Strasbourg was near the Rhine on the major route from Paris to both Germany and Switzerland and was a reputed republican stronghold, militantly political, and plagued with overcrowding and unemployment. Protestants comprised the main portion of the city's enlightened bourgeoisie and dominated its commerce and municipal council. A radical opposition to the Orleanist government comprised not only a host of Protestants but some Catholics, as well as a number of German and Polish refugees with close ties to German liberals and French republicans. The garrison at Strasbourg had been alone in refusing orders disbanding Napoleon's army after Waterloo. When reservists had rebelled against the 1823 Bourbon intervention in Spain, Strasbourg liberals had organized a regency council to "joyfully welcome the august heir," Napoleon II. From 1830 to 1836, reports of trouble in the Strasbourg garrison reached the war ministry every year except 1832. And in that year the 16th infantry regiment, then in Paris but at Strasbourg in 1836, earned a reputation for troublesome activity against the government. The garrison's record was, to say the least, one of questionable loyalty.

Louis Napoleon in Strasbourg streets? Despite banishment from France? Who were his supporters? Colonel Claude Vaudrey, the garrison's second in command, controlled all Strasbourg artillery. Could he be a Bonaparte accomplice? Was garrison commander General Voirol, another old soldier of the Empire, one too? Why had Prefect Augustin Choppin-d'Arnouville not alerted the government? Were all of these collaborators? Were they captives? Murky as the fog between Strasbourg and Paris, the truncated telegram provided no reassurance, no hint of opposition to Louis Napoleon.

King and cabinet huddled apprehensively all night. There was none of the arrogant scoffing which came later, but a serious conjecturing and weighing of probabilities. They discussed measures to be taken and prepared instructions. Contributing to the unsettling situation was more disturbing news. The Chartres hussars had revolted at the village of Vendôme, southwest of Paris, at the same hour and on the same day, 6:00 a.m., Sunday, October 30. Could this be part of a larger revolt?

Guizot sensitively noticed the sadness of the king, "always obliged to be on guard against many enemies." The Orleanist Louis Philippe seemed to unite men only in opposition to the Bourbons; otherwise incessant and irreconcilable political differences permeated and harassed his government. He had reigned only six years, uncomfortably the same as the Bourbon he had replaced. Would he now be supplanted by a Bonaparte?

Agitated, the entire royal family paced the palace all night. Queen Marie Amélie, the king's sister, Adelaide, and even the children, drifted in and out of the emergency cabinet meeting. Uneasy, they longed for more information and consolation, but the crestfallen Louis Philippe could give them neither. After all, no French monarch's son had succeeded to the throne for two hundred years.

The king's eldest son, Ferdinand, Duke of Chartres and Orleans, prepared to ride towards Strasbourg. No ordinary emissary would suffice; a Bonaparte prince necessitated an Orleanist prince. Two years younger than Louis Napoleon, the twenty-six-year-old duke had been born in exile at the height of the Empire. Now his proscribed Paris-born rival was causing "dreadful uncertainties" and distress. "The whole of last night we sat up without news," he confided to his brother, the Duke of Nemours, whose absence he wearily envied. Ferdinand's nineteen-year-old sister, Clementine, echoed this apprehension. An air of crisis, she wrote, animated the Tuileries and its courtyard. Officers and aides-de-camp strode around in anxious anticipation and the carriages of ministers stood ready. Horses, saddled for an undetermined destination, pranced restlessly in the dark.

For eleven hours Louis Philippe and his ministers speculated and irresolutely drifted into numbed inactivity. Guizot reported that "We fell asleep from fatigue and woke up again impatient." The idea of Louis Napoleon in the streets of Strasbourg had produced an unsettling "fickleness and a tendency to waver." In historian Albert Guérard's apt description of the scene, the ministers "eyed one another with misgivings and wondered whether their coats could stand being turned once more." Most had served Napoleon. Why not accept his heir?

• • •

Charles Louis Napoleon Bonaparte, the cause of consternation at this emergency meeting, was no stranger to the men at the Tuileries. His grandfathers Beauharnais and Bonaparte had mingled with fellow aristocrats at Versailles; his father and three of his uncles had occupied European thrones. His grandmothers were, of course, Napoleon's wife Josephine and Letitzia, the mother of his father Louis as well as Napoleon. His parents were Hortense de Beauharnais, daughter of the Empress Josephine, and Louis Bonaparte, brother of the emperor. Though the young Louis Napoleon was born during their brief reign (1806-1810) as the monarchs of Holland, he was never in the Dutch kingdom while they were on its throne.

Though incompatible otherwise, the young couple was prolific. Despite disliking each other, Hortense proved herself an adequate queen, producing three sons in six years. The eldest was born October 10, 1802 and died May 5, 1807. The second son was born October 11, 1804. The youngest, Louis Napoleon, born prematurely in Paris on April 20, 1808, happened to be the first Bonaparte prince born after establishment of the Empire. On this occasion Hortense's chamberlain, Count Bylandt, traveled from Paris to Amsterdam to notify Louis of the birth of his new son. The king wrote a touching letter to his wife and announced the event to Dutch citizens assembled under his balcony. When the queen sent word to Napoleon at Bayonne, he had salutes fired all along the Spanish border and named the child Charles Napoleon. King Louis defiantly inserted his own name between those of his father and brother; the new prince was thus Charles Louis Napoleon Bonaparte. The proud emperor was his uncle, step-grandfather and godfather.

Napoleon took a special interest in the children of Hortense and Louis. Even before they were born he told Josephine: "We may never have children. I brought up Louis myself; I look on him as a son. Your daughter is what you cherish most on earth. Their children shall be our children. We will adopt them, and this adoption will console us for not having any of our own." However, in April of 1807 King Louis resentfully wrote Hortense that they must "make common cause to keep the guardianship of our children and not allow them to be adopted by the Emperor or the Empress." Hortense curtly replied, "God is master of their fate and it is for Him to decide what that fate shall be." Napoleon was zealous regarding the safety of his little heirs and, during the 1809 Wagram campaign severely chastised Hortense for casually taking two of the children to Baden, "One hour after you receive this letter, send my two nephews to Strasbourg, to the Empress; they should never leave France . . . I repeat, lose not a moment in sending my nephews to Strasbourg . . .; they should never pass the bridge of Strasbourg." By the age of three, however, Louis Napoleon's destiny appeared doomed; his father had abdicated July 1, 1810, and his cousin, Napoleon's son, the King of Rome, had been born March 20, 1811. The Empire fell three years later. As Napoleon emotionally dismissed the Old Guard with his famous farewell, Louis was commemorating his sixth birthday. It was April 20, 1814 and his world had abruptly changed.

After Waterloo, the Bonapartes were banished from France by the law of January 12, 1816. This was to be later reinforced by laws of September 16, 1830 and April 10, 1832. Napoleon's son, François Joseph Charles, the King of Rome, became Franz Josef Karl. Given the title of Duke of Reichstadt, he was confined under Austrian control to a genteel life at Schonbrunn. Louis and Hortense legally separated in 1815; and the Bonaparte family scattered to Italy, Switzerland, southern Germany, England and America. The young Louis and his mother, now known as the Duchess of Saint Leu, were callously harassed from one town to another: Geneva, Aix-les-Bains, Berne, Zurich, and Augsburg, while his father and older brother settled in Florence. For thirty-three years the emperor's nephew would legally be on French soil only when imprisoned.

Hortense and her son eventually settled in Switzerland at the small chateau of Arenenberg, a few miles west of Constance on the Swiss-German border. Here she thoroughly nourished her son in the Napoleonic Legend. More formal and traditional education came from tutors and the gymnasium in Augsburg. As a summer volunteer in the Swiss army he also studied artillery and military engineering at the Military Academy at Thun where his instructors were two veterans of the Empire, Colonels Dufour and Fournier.

Louis Napoleon was only thirteen years old when Napoleon Bonaparte died but already was imbued with a sense of the unique importance of his heritage, writing his mother, "when I ….think of this great man I seem to feel his shadow within me." Nine years later when the 1830 revolution erupted in Paris, he became in effect third in line as the Bonaparte heir. He was actually fifth, after the King of Rome, his uncle Joseph, his father Louis, and his older brother. Pragmatically, however, his father and Joseph were not serious pretenders. Louis was an invalid and Joseph had no sons. The tricolor once again became the French flag and, also, the revolutionary colors in Italy, where most of the exiled Bonapartes had settled. During the interregnum after the death of Pope Pius VII on November 30, 1830, Louis Napoleon was in Rome and an uprising was planned to proclaim him regent for his cousin, the King of

Rome. Deeming the plot serious, officers of the papal army expeditiously escorted him across the border into Tuscany—and into the midst of fellow agitators, collaborating Bonapartes, and former officers of his uncle, the ex-Viceroy of Italy, Eugene de Beauharnais. After several months of intense revolutionary activity Louis Napoleon and Hortense barely escaped capture by the Austrian army and, ignoring French laws banishing the family, illegally crossed into France. His elder brother, meanwhile, had succumbed to measles on March 17, 1831, and Louis was seriously ill with a fever.

The presence in Paris of Louis Napoleon, now second in line as the Bonaparte contender, flustered the beleaguered Orleanist regime. Louis Philippe's minister of war, Marshal Nicolas Soult, formerly Napoleon's chief of staff in 1815, admitted that his appearance in France was "very serious news." Louis Napoleon, when only seven years old, had been with Soult and the emperor the day before they left for Waterloo. Now, only the emperor's son—virtually a prisoner in Vienna—was a closer claimant for the French throne and the new king was especially apprehensive about Bonaparte heirs.

On April 23, 1831, for the first time in sixteen years, Louis Napoleon and Hortense entered Paris. Rather conspicuously, they stayed at the Hotel de Hollande, number sixteen Rue de la Paix—overlooking the Place Vendôme, site of Bonapartist rallies. Hortense requested an audience with Louis Philippe while Louis wrote the monarch stating that he wished to serve in the French army "as a simple soldier." Weary of furtiveness and gently audacious, Hortense conceded to Casimir Périer, the king's autocratic minister, "You have the right to arrest me. It would be just." His prudent reply, "Legal, yes. Just, no."

Hortense met with the king on Tuesday evening, April 26, to discuss the general ban on Bonapartes and especially her own status and travel plans. Meanwhile, despite still being ill, Louis Napoleon was talking with principal leaders of the republican party.

According to Casimir Périer, he boldly discussed methods to topple Louis Philippe. Although both Hortense and her traveling companion, Valerie Masuyer, defensively denied this allegation, it has a ring of truth.

May 5, 1831, the tenth anniversary of Napoleon's death, became another day of anxiety for Louis Philippe. The young Alexandre Dumas stirred Parisian emotions with his play *Napoleon Bonaparte, or Thirty Years of French History*" And Daguerre's diorama, a dramatic tableau representing Napoleon's tomb at St. Helena, enjoyed great popularity—attracting even the royal family. On the 5th of May, two infantry battalions quietly appeared on the Place Vendôme and, according to Guizot, so did Louis Napoleon. The crowd shouted "Vive l'Empéreur," "Vive Napoléon II," and crowned the four statuary eagles with garlands of flowers. Riots broke out.

During his meeting with Hortense, Louis Philippe had alternated between "reminiscing gaily" and being ill at ease, recalling his own life as a refugee. While teaching at Reichenau in 1793 he had been within sight of Arenenberg. Remembering "inconceivable persecution" and also the "policies and passions" of émigrés, he declared to the former queen that "Soon there will be no more exiles; I want none during my reign." The events of May 5, however, were especially disquieting and he judiciously had the Bonapartes pressured out of Paris the next day. They had been in the French capital two weeks. Louis Napoleon later confided, "The people are Bonapartists. If I had . . . appeared at the Place Vendôme and shouted, 'Vive Napoléon II,' everyone would have followed me." That was exactly what the Orleanist government feared. As for his request to serve in the army, it was declared possible only if he gave up his name, using that of St. Leu instead – a decision he found infuriating. His real reason for offering to serve was that he felt it would be better to be within France rather than abroad whenever the Orleanist regime fell, an event he deemed likely.

Hastily leaving for England, Hortense, Louis Napoleon, and

Valerie Masuyer arrived in London in mid-May. Bonapartes and friends supportively surrounded them. Louis Napoleon's cousin, Achille Murat, elder son of Joachim Murat and Caroline Bonaparte, had just arrived from America with his wife, a great-niece of George Washington. Also welcoming them to England was another cousin, Christine-Egypta Bonaparte, now Lady Dudley Stuart, daughter of Lucien Bonaparte and his first wife, Christine Boyer. After three socially active months, on August 7, the entourage left Dover for Boulogne and a sentimental side-trip to the Colonne de la Grande Armée. Dutifully skirting Paris, they made brief detours to Joseph's former chateau, Mortefontaine, and Josephine's Malmaison.

Within a year after returning to Arenenberg, Louis Napoleon became the primary Bonaparte contender when, after a lingering lung disease, Napoleon's only legal son died on July 22, 1832. Although the two cousins had not seen each other for eighteen years, Louis Napoleon had written him a touchingly affectionate letter during his illness. The letter, unfortunately, never reached its destination as it was intercepted and retained by Prince Metternich.

Joseph had been in America for seventeen years; but when he learned of the serious state of the King of Rome's health, the sixty-four year old former King of Naples and of Spain decided to make another unpleasant trans-Atlantic crossing. Thus, four months after their nephew's death, Joseph and Lucien Bonaparte held a family conference in London, with Louis Napoleon representing his invalid father. The older Bonapartes now indicated, at least for public display, that they wanted no part in disturbing the French political system. Earlier, however, on October 9, 1830 Joseph had written both Metternich and the Austrian emperor, supporting the King of Rome as Napoleon II and protesting Louis Philippe's ascension to the throne of France. Lucien had twice vainly requested passports to see Napoleon's son, camouflaging any dynastic ambitions by stating, "I consider the right of Napoleon as that of yesterday, the right of Louis Philippe as that of today."

Despite such public pronouncements, those dissatisfied with

Orleanists sought out the Bonaparte brothers. Republican leaders Geoffrey Cavaignac, Joseph Gurnard, and Jules Bastide crossed the English Channel to confer with them. As early as 1825 Lafayette had told Joseph he would work for the succession of Napoleon II. Seven years later he was disillusioned with Louis Philippe and believed another revolution inevitable. In July of 1832 after disturbances at General Lamarque's funeral in June, he advised Louis Napoleon, "Seize the first opportunity to return to France because the government cannot maintain control and your name is the only popular one." After Lafayette's death, May 20, 1834, Armand Carrel became the republican leader and echoed Lafayette: the name of Napoleon Bonaparte was the only one powerful enough to excite the sympathy of the French people.

• • •

October of 1836 merged into November and another anniversary of 18 Brumaire. As All Saints' Day dawned at the Tuileries, Louis Philippe's ministers pondered their options, their deliberations themselves an homage to the power of the Napoleonic Legend.

Chapter Two

The Napoleonic Legend

Napoleon Bonaparte's most robust heir, the Napoleonic Legend, was born during the Return from Elba and matured on Saint Helena. Sturdier by far than the King of Rome, it cast the emperor in a whole new light. He had become the father of liberty, enemy of absolutism, symbol of revolt, champion of self determination, and a proponent of democracy. In exile Napoleon had written, "My dictatorship would have ended, my constitutional rule would have begun. . . . I asked for twenty years. Destiny gave me thirteen." Chateaubriand ruefully observed that he had metamorphosed into virtually a god and that France had "bowed, wept, and forgave. The world belongs to Napoleon....Living, he failed to win the world; dead, he possesses it."

The Legend surged after the emperor's death in 1821. Memoirs appeared in bookstalls and Napoleonic bric-a-brac scattered throughout France, lithographs, engravings, medals, busts, battle scenes, napkin rings, cane heads, pocket knives. His portrait was placed beside those of Christ and the Virgin Mary. In 1828 and 1829, the department of the Seine reported the worried Bourbon view that all such memorabilia were "seditious objects". However, even at the Ecole Polytechnique whose patron was the Duke of Angoulême, son of King Charles X, a major topic of discussion was Bonaparte's career.

The 1820s were a formidable quagmire for the Bourbons. Replacing Napoleon's vigorous and imperious stride, Louis XVIII was a sixty-year-old invalid who moved about in a wheelchair. The whole Bourbon Restoration appeared to be a gerontocracy of "seven or eight thousand asthmatic, gouty, paralytic eligible candidates with enfeebled faculties."

Liberalism, like Napoleon, was progressive and vital. Bourbon and Orleanist policies—the status quo in France—appeared negative. French liberals fused the Napoleonic magic to their cause and republicans incorporated him into their anti-government rhetoric. When sovereigns retracted promises, the emperor became liberalism's hero in Poland, Italy, and southern Germany. Above all, he epitomized hostility towards those restored monarchs who were supported mainly by foreign bayonets.

Weary of dullness by the late 1820s, younger romantics in various phases—rebellion, nostalgic attachment to the past, a quest for the dramatically picturesque—turned from the Bourbons and embraced the Legend, accepting the liberal-Bonapartist standard. With them Napoleon's career was a favorite literary theme. Elder romantics, however – Chateaubriand, Lamennais, Lamartine, Vigny, Michelet – remained hostile to Napoleon-worship; and after 1870 republicans generally regretted that before 1848 so many of their number had been Bonapartists.

The Bonapartists' poet laureate was Pierre de Béranger (1780-1857). Thirty-four years old when the Empire fell, he scorned and mocked the Bourbons. He wrote of and to the people and especially about Napoleon. From *The Garret*, he heard the "far boom of artillery roll—Napoleon had vanquished; Marengo was won! . . . Mighty France our one theme, and the Laurels she wore! . . . Ah, give me my youth and a garret once more!" Imprisoned briefly in 1821 and again in 1828 in "his Majesty's snug cell" for offending the Bourbon monarchy, Béranger's "ribald pen" continued to glorify his hero.

The poignant *Granny's Reminiscences of Napoleon*, declared that "His fame shall never pass away!" On winter nights around the hearth, children begged for a story about the man with the little black hat and the big grey coat. "Although they say he did us harm,

Our love this cannot dim; Come, Granny, talk of him to us; Come, Granny, talk of him." In *Memoires of the People*, Béranger reiterated, "They will talk of His glory under thatched roofs, for ages."

When the grandson of the future Charles X was born in 1820, Béranger composed a touching and prophetic *Birthday Letter* from the King of Rome. He had Napoleon's son informing the new Bourbon prince that lilies had once yielded to bees and cautioned him about the shifting sands of adulation. "At the time of my birth, kings crowded their homage to pay; Round my cot cringed the lords of the earth—And yet I'm an exile today." As the Duke of Bordeaux's christening became a theme of minstrals, the Duke of Reichstadt described his own baptismal water: "They sent to the Jordan for mine—And yet I'm an exile today." He had a sceptre instead of a rattle, a crown instead of a cap: "From a Pontiff 'twas taken away, . . . And Yet I'm an exile today." Warning that generals would desert him, he recalled, "To my sire they were bound by an oath he believed they could never betray; All was staked on the oft-vaunted troth—And yet I'm an exile today!" Ten years later, this Bourbon heir joined his Bonaparte counterpart in exile.

Béranger's *Old Flag* recalled "many and many a glorious fight" before it became "a worn out veteran's single prize." But even though the eagle "in the dust lies low," Béranger offered hope to Frenchmen—and a threat to Louis XVI's brother. Soldiers, as citizens, would "be found on Duty's side" and would restore the old flag, "my pride, my hope, my all." Although Béranger never served in the army, he ended his poem, "Come wipe away a soldier's tear . . . Can Heaven my humble prayer deny? No, no, once more—ah! Glorious thought, I'll see you float before I die!" And he did, for the last twenty-seven years of his life.

In 1820 the average edition for books of poetry was 500 copies. But in 1821, to the consternation of the Bourbons, eleven thousand copies of Béranger's collected poems sold within a week. Five years later an illustrated edition sold even more. The Napoleonic Legend and the poet's catchy stanzas permeated France; twenty-five million voices repeated his refrains. In 1829 the frustrated government helplessly ordered street singers to stop glorifying Napoleon in song.

Never as popular during his lifetime as Béranger, Marie Henri Beyle (1783-1842) also had a lifelong fascination with Napoleon. Adopting the pen name of Stendhal, he remained loyal even when it was impolitic. He arrived in Paris at age sixteen on November 10, 1799, the day after his idol became first consul. Unlike Béranger, he was close to the emperor, traveling with Napoleon's headquarters staff. In 1800 he witnessed the battle of Marengo; in 1812 he served as commissioner of war supplies and participated in the retreat from Moscow. He was also an auditor of the council of state. In 1817 he audaciously dedicated his *Histoire de la peinture en Italie* to "His Majesty Napoleon the Great"—"the greatest of all existing monarchs"—as if he were still reigning. Stendhal ruefully observed in his autobiographical *Life of Henry Brulard* that "I fell with Napoleon in April 1814."

In *Le Rouge et le Noir*, published in 1830, Stendhal's Julien Sorel rose from humble origins and, like Napoleon, shook the established order. Both Stendhal and his hero Julian symbolized the individual against society, the Napoleonic red contrasted with the Restoration black. Correcting proofs when the 1830 revolution erupted, the sight of the tricolors renewed Stendhal's hope. On November 6 he left Paris for Trieste after Louis Philippe had appointed him consul at that Austrian-controlled city. Prince Metternich, however, suspected that he was associated with the Carbonari in Milan and would not accept the forty-seven year old author-diplomat. The Austrian minister was probably correct. While waiting for further instructions from Paris, Stendhal was on the periphery of revolutions involving Bonapartes in Modena, Bologna, Forli, and Ravenna. To the dismay of papal authorities, Louis Philippe next accredited him to Civitavecchia, a small port near Rome. He spent a week in Florence, home of ex-King Louis Bonaparte, before leisurely arriving at his new post on April 17, 1831.

After becoming disillusioned with the Orleanist regime,

Stendhal took an extended leave of absence which, thanks to the generosity of Molé, was to last three years. Returning to Paris in May 1836, he met the Countess de Montijo de Guzman and her daughter, the future Empress Eugenie. His conversations with them about Napoleon were brimming with his usual enthusiasm.

At the time Louis Napoleon was planning his Strasbourg coup, Stendhal began literary projects and journeys with "an almost feverish quality" of activity. He traveled to Bourges, Tours, Le Havre, Rouen, Bordeaux, Toulouse, Carcassonne, Montpellier, Marseilles, Toulon and Valence, as well as Bern, Basel, Baden, Mainz, Frankfurt, Rotterdam, Amsterdam, the Hague and Brussels. He also frequently changed addresses in Paris. However, in November 1836, shortly after Louis Napoleon's abortive coup, he settled down and resumed writing his *Memoirs on Napoleon*, a project started twenty years earlier. This and his *Life of Napoleon* were published after his death, when a Stendhal renaissance occurred. By the time Louis Napoleon arrived in New York in April of 1837, Stendhal had abruptly changed his primary focus and wrote for the *Revue des Deux Mondes* a series of stories with similar themes: exceptional daring and defiance of the law.

In 1838 when Louis Napoleon began his exile in England, Stendhal wrote *The Charterhouse of Parma*, dashing it off in fifty-two days and finishing it on Christmas. By early April 1839, the novel was printed. The title page simply identified him as "the author of *The Red and the Black*." The young hero, Fabrice del Dongo, was idealistic, high-spirited, impulsive, bold, enthusiastic, generous, noble, daring, eager, willing to risk disgrace—and an ardent admirer of Napoleon. This description of Fabrice, "the nephew," could also have been appropriate for Louis Napoleon..

Almost twenty years younger than Stendhal, Victor Hugo (1802-1885) also made significant contributions to the Legend. Although his mother was a royalist, his father was a Napoleonic general that accompanied Joseph Bonaparte from Naples to Madrid, becoming governor of Madrid, a count of the Empire and

King Joseph's confidential adviser. Joining Napoleon during the Hundred Days, he held the frontier fortress at Thionville until September 13, 1815 – three months after Waterloo. When only nine years old, Victor Hugo had participated in festivities at the birth of the King of Rome. Accordingly, his attachment to the memory of Napoleon came naturally.

The Two Islands, Corsica and St. Helena, published in 1825, gave a nod to the Bourbons, who had sustained him with a pension, yet also boldly proclaimed, "Fame to Napoleon! Fame be to the Lord Supreme! God's self upon his brow had placed the diadem." The Greek War of Independence inspired *Les Orientales*, defiantly declaring that "Napoleon, dazzling and sombre, stands on the threshold of the century." *Hernani*, a romantic drama first produced in 1830 at the Theatre Francais, became a political event and a virtual rehearsal for revolution. Whenever the actor said "Charlemagne," the French seemed to hear "Napoleon."

When revolution did erupt in July 1830, Hugo preferred Napoleon's son to Louis Philippe. A few months later he wrote his second *Ode to the Column* in which the twin gods were Napoleon and Liberty. In 1831 he daringly confided to Joseph Bonaparte, his father's old patron, "I believe in the future of your nephew . . . . But it is good sometimes that the hand of man should help the natural course of events . . . . All the generous youth of France will rally to his cause—and with that generous youth of France, obscure though I be, I have some influence." Ten months later when the emperor's son died, Hugo penned an *Ode to the King of Rome* and sent a copy to Alexandre Dumas, then visiting Louis Napoleon at Arenenberg.

Honoré de Balzac (1799-1850), a teen-ager like Hugo in 1815, kept on his desk a small statue of the emperor. Across it he etched, "What he failed to accomplish by the sword I shall achieve by the pen." His admiration for Napoleon provoked Sainte-Beuve to fret, "I wish that he might have put aside once and for all the thought of comparing himself to his hero or childishly emulating him." He acknowledged, however, that Balzac "knew and felt the imperial epoch with the clearsightedness and special penetration of childhood which was later complemented by reflection."

Napoleon permeated Balzac's pages. Colonel Chabert, wounded at Eylau, mourned, "When I think that Napoleon is on Saint Helena, nothing in this world seems to matter any more." Gondrin, the only pontoneer surviving the Beresina crossing, returned without a medal, without a pension, and became a mere roadmender. Yet he felt only adoration for the emperor. Captain Genestas, another veteran, lamented, "We no longer have our father."

Balzac's private Goguelat, soldier turned postman, gathered peasants around him and told them about this child of God: "Volleys of grapeshot and showers of bullets" killed ordinary soldiers—but not Napoleon. Although the plague in Syria felled others, he remained "as fresh as a rose." Despite England's blockade of Egypt, Napoleon had "a star of his own." He eluded them in "a little cockleshell, a mere nothing of a skiff," and returned to France "in the twinkling of an eye." Whenever he spoke "something in his words made our hearts burn within us." He commanded such loyalty that dying men raised up to salute and cry, "Long live the Emperor."

Peasants were spellbound by Goguelat's version of the Legend. The Pope called Napoleon "My son;" Mehemet's cousin in Egypt called him "My dear Father." Church bells rang "for God and Napoleon." He made "bridges, palaces, roads, scholars, festivals, laws, fleets, and harbors." So much gold poured in he "could have paved the whole of France with five-franc pieces if the fancy had taken him."

Parisians betrayed him. "Like Jesus Christ before the crucifixion, he thought himself forsaken by God." Then he took "enough poison to kill a regiment but it had no effect whatever upon him. Another marvel! He discovered that he was immortal." With "a show of his hat" and three words, "Here I am," he returned to France—"the greatest miracle God ever worked." Like Jesus he was betrayed and imprisoned. Balzac's peasants sullenly denounced Bourbons for reporting the death of Napoleon, "the child of God." They continued to drink to "the Little Corporal" eight years after he had died, and they solemnly toasted him with "Vive l'Empéreur!"

Like Balzac's peasants, fifteen years after the emperor was buried, Edgar Quinet's pen proclaimed, "He is not dead! He is not dead!" Quinet (1803-1875) portrayed a Prometheus, destroyer of the old regime, incarnation of the revolution, martyr of democracy. His choir queried and cajoled, "Men of Lodi . . . of Marengo, where are you? Rise from the earth; you retired too soon. Come accomplish the task your children lack the heart to achieve."

Heinrich Heine (1797-1856) also gave homage to the man of Lodi and Marengo. When the teen-age Heine saw Napoleon at Dusseldorf, "the Emperor, the Emperor, the Great Emperor" appeared to him "a vision of golden summer" and his countenance, "the complexion found on marble heads of Greeks and Romans, his features as nobly proportioned as those of ancient statues." In 1832 Heine rhetorically noted that the emperor's picture was in every French hut. He also remarked that "Outside of France few people realize with how much devotion the French still regard Napoleon . . . . 'Napoleon' is a magic word to the French; it electrifies and stuns them. In his name a thousand cannons sleep, even in the column on the Place Vendôme. And the Tuileries will tremble when these cannons awake . . . ." Heine saw a child of three in a dark and deserted alley "lisping the glories of the great Emperor." Cripples did not beg in the name of the Lord, but implored, "In the name of Napoleon, give me a sou."

Theophile Gautier's *Veterans of the Old Guard* subsequently reflected the same adulation that Heine had so adroitly captured. He wrote of five soldiers of the Grand Army celebrating the 1840 return of Napoleon from St. Helena with a faithful pilgrimage to the Vendôme Column——as if going to God's altar.

Although only a five-year-old child in 1815, Alfred de Musset

(1810-1857) felt the pervasiveness of utter catastrophe after Waterloo. Growing up under the soberness of the restored Bourbons, he yearned for the joy and vitality of the Empire when his father had served as an administrator. "God made the sun for this man . . . and they called it the Sun of Austerlitz," he wrote in *Confession of a Child of the Century*. Napoleon himself made the sunlight, dispelled all clouds, gave France a "spotless sky," and shook the world. Crowns of kings vacillated; "raising their hands to steady them, they found only their hair, bristling with terror."

Musset bitterly lashed out at the treatment of France as a pariah nation. When Napoleon fell "the half-dead powers rose up from their sick beds and, stretching out their hooked legs, all the royal spiders tore Europe into shreds, and made themselves Harlequin coats from Caesar's purple mantle." France, the "widow of Caesar," stumbled into extreme lassitude. "He who had become the centre of our lives has been laid low, and existence without him seems unprofitable and stale." Musset's generation, the poet gloomily regretted, would never experience the "snows of Moscow and the sunlight of the pyramids."

Musset's contemporaries vicariously relived the Egyptian and Russian campaigns through the voluminous historical writing of Adolfe Thiers (1797-1877). An impressionable teen-ager during the later Empire, Thiers' narratives sympathized with popular governments and dramatized Napoleon as the savior of France. His work sold hundreds of thousands of copies with much the same public effect as the *Marseillaise*. Regarded by Marshal Soult as a "tiresome little fidget," he became a major opponent of Guizot and when in power promoted an aggressive foreign policy.

Equally as invigorating, artists enhanced the literary Legend by portraying the glory and grandeur of Napoleon. Jacques Louis David (1748-1825) dominated French painting from 1789 to 1815. A regicide later banished by the Bourbons, he was captivated by Bonaparte's dynamic personality and at age fifty-one became court painter to the first consul. Elevating him to "first painter of the Empire," Napoleon temptingly promised, "For every historical picture you paint you shall receive 100,000 francs;" David responded with *Bonaparte Crossing the Saint Bernard*, the *Coronation of Napoleon*, and *Distribution of the Eagles*. In mutual admiration, the emperor praised him and David predicted that posterity would exclaim, "What men and what an Emperor!"

Antoine Jean Gros (1771-1835), David's pupil, captivated Napoleon and the world by painting him, sword in one hand and standard in the other, at the bridge of Arcola. Gross was rewarded, not by 100,000 francs, but by a military commission to depict war at close range. This he did: *Battle of the Pyramids*, *Napoleon at Jaffa*, the *Battle of Aboukir*, the *Battle of Eylau*, the *Conquest of Madrid*, the *Battle of Wagram*, and Napoleon pointing to a list of his victories.

Yet another disciple of David, Baron François Gérard (1770-1837) also significantly contributed to the Legend. After early portraits of both Josephine and Napoleon, he captured Napoleon in two memorable December 2 events: resplendent in his coronation robes and a year later victorious at the battle of Austerlitz. He became a court painter under Louis XVIII and adapting to the Orleanists, he also painted Louis Philippe. Dominique Ingres (1780-1867), also a pupil of David, represented a radiant emperor, crowned with laurel, ascending to heaven. Jean Louis Gericault, Pierre Paul Prud'hon and other talented artists immortalized the great grey coat, the petite chapeau, the lock of hair on the forehead, and the hypnotic eyes.

After the 1830 revolution, theatrical performances gave Napoleon yet another dimension.. Any play concerning "the great man" became an enormous success. The public never got enough. Within four months, from the end of August to the end of December 1830, at least twelve plays about his life opened in Paris: *Bonaparte at Brienne*; *Bonaparte, Lieutenant of the Artillery*; *Crossing the Saint-Bernard Pass*; *Josephine, or the Return from Wagram*; *Napoleon at Berlin*; *Napoleon, the Emperor*; *Fourteen Years of the Life of Napoleon; The Empire and the Hundred Days; The Willow of St. Helena; Schoenbrunn and St. Helena, Malmaison and St. Helena; The Son of the Man;* and *The Man of the Century.*

Various actors imitated him in every stage of his career. Playing the role of Napoleon so successfully the great man himself seemed to be on stage, Gobert stirred each evening's audience into a frenzy. When Alexandre Dumas' *Napoleon Bonaparte* opened at the Odeon, the actor representing Sir Hudson Lowe was so convincing he had to have police protection to keep him from being stoned on his way home. Though Dumas was the son of an impoverished but respected Napoleonic general, the play so irritated Louis Philippe that Dumas lost his position as the king's assistant librarian.

The Legend excited disparate social classes and societies. In 1819 the Hawaiian prince Kouakine surprised the explorer Freycinet by his curiosity about Napoleon. Ten years later an Inca chief in Patagonia welcomed the naturalist Alcide d'Orbigny and eagerly queried, Was he from the country of Napoleon? Had he seen him? Had he spoken to him? Returning from sea after the revolutionary July days, a Boulogne fisherman spotted the tricolor and shouted, "I knew that He was not dead!" No name was needed. "He" could only be Napoleon. An Imperial Guard captain who had been at Elba commissioned François Rudé to sculpt an impressive statue of the emperor reclining in death; it was placed on the devoted captain's tomb with the epitaph: "Here lies a soldier of Napoleon I." By including the roman numeral, he anticipated another Bonaparte reign.

The most important disciple of the Legend was probably Louis Napoleon. During his youth and teenage years he had been continuously exposed to stories about Napoleon as Hortense systematically imbued him with the mystique of his uncle and the Empire. Supplementing her efforts were many veterans of the Empire who had also settled in Switzerland. Her home at Arenenberg was a magnet attracting a continuous parade of impressive visitors. Their vivid and nostalgic recollections comprised a heady atmosphere for the young nephew of the larger than life emperor. He became completely imbued with the Legend.

Louis Philippe, however, was unwittingly, perhaps, the Legend's greatest ally. Even his children, who drew pictures of Napoleon "all over the place," acknowledged "the greatest admiration for the great warrior." On an official naval visit to Corsica in 1831, Louis Philippe's third son, the Duke of Joinville, then only thirteen years old, toured the Bonaparte house in Ajaccio and impulsively asked for a red armchair from the room of Napoleon's birth. Signor André Ramolino, a cousin of Madame Letitzia, obligingly gave it to him.

To some, Louis Philippe seemed to indicate a "feverish and silly jealousy" of Napoleon's family; but the events of 1848 were to prove this "jealousy" to be well-founded and certainly not "silly". The king clearly understood the power of the great name. Accused of pandering to Bonapartists even before he came to power, after the revolution he surrounded himself with those his immediate predecessors had ostracized: imperial officers, ministers, marshals, bureaucrats, and even Count Alexandre Walewski, the illegitimate son of the fallen emperor. Rhetorically, Marshal Macdonald handed the new king his crown, Oudinot his sceptre, Mortier his sword. Maurice Etienne Gérard, who had rallied to the emperor in 1815, became the minister of war on August 11, 1830; a week later Louis Philippe elevated him to marshal, a promotion Napoleon earlier had planned. After resigning because of health, Gérard went on to capture Antwerp and later served again as minister of war and president of the council of ministers. In 1852 he became a senator of the Second Empire. Marshal Soult, one of Napoleon's' ablest commanders, served Louis Philippe with particular distinction. He was twice minister of war, twice also president of the council of ministers and once minister of foreign affairs. He was widely revered and in 1847 named Marshal-General of France, a supreme distinction awarded previously only to Turenne, Villars, and Saxe.

The Legend quickened when major military posts went to Napoleon's old commanders. All but two of these had supported

Napoleon during the Hundred Days. Almost forty percent of Louis Philippe's newly appointed generals had been nobles of the Empire. Eighteen of twenty ministerial positions went to the emperor's officials, twelve of whom had participated in the Hundred Days. Six of these lived to see the Second Empire and five of these served Napoleon III. Over one-third of the prefects and procurer-generals appointed in August and September of 1830 had previously served Napoleon. An Austrian diplomat recorded in his journal on September 3, 1830, that "Adherents of Napoleon II become stronger every day" and noted that French leaders were all "creatures of Napoleon" merely serving Louis Philippe to prevent anarchy and to paralyze republicans, waiting only for a favorable moment to dethrone this newcomer and to proclaim Napoleon II.

Louis Philippe even turned to the emperor's relatives. He summoned General Charles de Flahaut—Talleyrand's son, Napoleon's aide-de-camp and Hortense's former lover—and sent him as envoy extraordinary and minister plenipotentiary to the King of Prussia. Nineteen year old Auguste de Morny—Hortense and Flauhaut's illegitimate son, Talleyrand's grandson and Louis Napoleon's half-brother—served in an elite lancers regiment. Morny had been raised by Flauhaut's mother, Madame de Souza, who had protected the exiled Louis Philippe in 1794, generating brief speculation that they might marry. Walewski served in the London embassy during the early 1830s and, later, became Orleanist ambassador to the sultan. He was to play a prominent role later in the Second Empire.

By early 1831 imperial officials, Napoleonic nobles, and veterans of the Empire represented almost half of the chamber of deputies. Of 191 members of the chamber of peers in 1831, 112 had served Napoleon and he had ennobled 88. Of course, not all who had served Napoleon became Bonapartists. Many were career officials who could comfortably serve any regime that happened to be in power.

Working from Napoleon's maple desk, Louis Philippe tried to satisfy the bourgeois split personality: Don Quixote's love of glory and Sancho Panza's love of hearth, slippers and newspaper. The tricolor was again the national flag, the *Marseillaise* jubilantly reverberated once again, and the mint struck one hundred sixty five medals representing memorable deeds during Napoleon's reign.

Only a few months after Louis Philippe became king, the chamber of deputies received a petition for the return of Napoleon's remains from St. Helena. The architect of "the most brilliant era of our history," must be honored. "His last request to be buried by the banks of the Seine must be respected." The pleas of popular General Lamarque were particularly impassioned. Napoleon's name was powerful. His memory was worshipped. His body must be returned, escorted by the tears of his old companions in arms. The chamber agreed.

Napoleon's statue, cast from cannon and destroyed by the Bourbons, was replaced on the Vendôme column and the king saluted the emperor in a great ceremony. The Arc de Triomphe, which still stands as a supreme monument to Napoleon, was begun in 1806, and finally completed and inaugurated on July 28, 1836. Complaining that Louis Philippe doted too much on Napoleon, Prince Metternich aptly fretted, "The 1830 regime is simply a housekeeping system for Bonapartism."

Chapter Three

The Problems of Louis Philippe and the Prospects of Louis Napoleon

Caught by surprise in July of 1830, Bonapartists, who had been among those fomenting discontent before the revolution, did not even have a visible candidate for the French throne. Belatedly, high-ranking Bonapartist officers enthusiastically formed committees and spread propaganda among all classes of the population. A former aide-de-camp of the emperor and future general, Gaspard Gourgaud, rallied fellow officers; and veterans of the Empire appeared in the front ranks of the revolutionaries shouting "Vive Napoléon! Vive l'Empéreur!" Dedicated followers appeared in the faubourgs and among the bourgeoisie, while among the workers evidence of devotion to the memory of Napoleon was overwhelming. Prefect of Police Henri Gisquet noted that "many hearts beat faster" at the hope of a Bonaparte once more leading France. If Napoleon's son had had the "ambitious designs" and "energetic resolution" of his father, and if he were not under Austrian control, he would "without doubt" have been a rallying force. On July 30, journalist Evariste Dumoulin produced a proclamation declaring "Napoleon II is the heir of your glory; he is our Emperor." Hoping for support from two members of the municipal commission, Mauguin and de Puyraveau, he appeared at the Hotel de Ville where he found his efforts neutralized by Lafayette who deftly locked him in a small room. It was all too little, too late.

Nevertheless, widespread popular support for a revived empire, only fifteen years after the Hundred Days, far exceeded that for republicans or Orleanists. Although they had lacked an effective leader, Bonapartists were generally encouraged by the July revolution. If not now, next time! Louis Napoleon, in particular, was impressed by the obvious adulation of his family which contrasted markedly with growing discontent with Louis Philippe.

Could Orleanists retain their new power? This seemed improbable. Louis Philippe reeled from physical threats, riots, and attempted insurrections, which "succeeded each other with something very like regularity." Even before he accepted the throne, thousands of Parisians "armed with all sorts of weapons," had confronted him. A "barrier of loaded guns, held horizontally" hemmed him in at the Hotel de Ville after he had met with Lafayette. A man "almost naked, armed with a halberd from one of the Swiss guards at the Tuileries, who leaped and danced while twirling the halberd about" led him with "frightening gestures" to the Palais Royal. Here insolent rabble drifted in and out before settling down for the night on the stairways. He was "guarded" by several hundred "vagabonds, prowling ruffians of the vilest kind, ragged scamps," who looked like robber chiefs, "frightening in their really shocking getup." There were surging crowds with lighted torches yelling "Death to Louis Philippe!" but despite the obvious threats to his personal security, he took the oath as King of the French on August 9, 1830. The beleaguered new monarch prudently transferred his wealth to his children and gave the order "to serve out ball cartridge, ball cartridge, do you hear?"

Revolutionary fervor slowed fitfully. Economic problems, revolutionary sects and ideas, an unleashed press, and declining respect for royalty prolonged the instability. Carriage and saddle workers, butchers, carpenters, locksmiths, machinists, port workers, stone masons, and bakery workers supported strikes, protests, and labor demonstrations from July to December of 1830. Time after time the National Guard under Lafayette's command responded to first one crisis, then another.

Violent demonstrations preceded and accompanied the December treason trials of the former ministers of Charles X. Sentences of life imprisonment rather than death added more flame to the turmoil. Massive concentrations of troops joined the National Guard in trying to control the mobs. Extraordinary security measures were taken. Mayors prepared to cut all church bell ropes to avoid the dreaded tocsin and the worried king and chamber pressured Lafayette's resignation. The tension in Paris generated rumors that Napoleon's son, heading an Austrian army on the French border, would announce a provisional Bonapartist government after the verdict.

Louis Philippe's devoted Guizot recorded "constant" insurrections and attempted assassinations. Reviewing the first six Orleanist years in thirty-four pages of his *History of France*, he discussed "frightful" and "deplorable" excesses, "perpetual" agitation, "disorderly fury," "warlike fermentation," "anarchy," "frequent fresh riots," and "incessant" conspiracies. Louis Blanc, Guizot's political protagonist, also catalogued "horrors, plots, and butcheries." Somewhat more restrained, Alexandre Dumas simply wrote, "There was no way possible for me to remain in Paris any longer. Riots swallowed up too much time and money."

In addition to internal crises, France was threatened with outside intervention while at the same time tempted to support continental revolts. Lafayette revealed documents from the portfolio of the Grand Duke Constantine, the brother of Tsar Nicholas, alleging that Russia had alerted troops, had sent a field marshal to Berlin for an offensive alliance, and had prepared the financing for a war against France. Louis Philippe was well aware of the tsar's propensity for ordering, "Saddle your horses, gentlemen!" whenever there was trouble in France. With a third of the French army engaged in Algeria, however, the king tempered impulses to intervene in the Belgian, Italian, and Polish revolutions. Casimir Périer ascribed to

"Peace at any price with the allied powers," and the minister of war went so far as to assert that peace was "preferable even to victory."

Not until January of 1831 did the Archbishop of Paris feel safe enough to emerge from hiding and resume his residence in the capital. Unfortunately for the prelate, he misjudged the brief Christmas tranquility. Several days of church-wrecking began in February and, to the applause of members of the National Guard, rioters attacked the archbishop's palace. After throwing furniture, books and priests' robes into the Seine, the mob methodically demolished the building.

Frenchmen were fearful, suspicious, uneasy and divided. The situation was deplorable. In March, seven months after Louis Philippe became king, riotous brawling continued to destroy order and street lamps. The "frightful cries" of unruly Parisians increased hourly at the Palais Royal until shouting crowds were edged back with bayonets and "murderous" combat by torch-light. Troops were bivouacked around fires, patrols moving through Paris in every direction. For some the unrest and instability were reminiscent of the months preceding 18 Brumaire. In April 1831, when Louis Napoleon was illegally in France, the mob "rolled and growled along the streets, like thunder in a long storm." The king hastily deleted the fleur-de-lys from his coat of arms and called Marshal Soult to the war ministry, overlooking allegations that the former commander of Napoleon's Imperial Guard was secretly cultivating partisans of Napoleon II.

Louis Philippe's lack of support became more and more apparent throughout 1831. Within two and one-half months, five juries acquitted conspirators accused of acts against the government. One young man, Evariste Gallois, toasted Louis Philippe with a dagger in his hand before two hundred people at a banquet. Arrested, he appeared before the court of assizes on June 15. Queried about his intentions, he admitted he would kill the king if he "ventured to depart from legal action." Furthermore, he told the court, "Everybody united in thinking that it will not be long before he acts illegally, if he has not already done so." The jury's verdict: "Not guilty."

In May 1831 government agents discovered a Strasbourg plot in behalf of the Duke of Reichstadt. The prefect of police eventually arrested Bonapartist conspirators but the government dared not give them a trial. It did, however, reinforce the laws banishing Bonapartes from France. Only two of the foreign conspirators involved were prosecuted and, to the government's despair, both were acquitted. Louis Philippe cautiously quieted publicity of Bonaparte threats, only reluctantly submitting to jury trials.

Between February and September of 1831, the Russian army was engaged in quelling revolution in Poland. When Warsaw fell, Parisians rioted in sympathy for the Polish people. Shops and theatres portentously closed and roaming mobs were shouting, "Vengeance! War on Russia!" By the end of September Louis Philippe abandoned the vulnerable Palais Royal and scurried to the fortified Tuileries, where he prudently had an underground escape passage constructed.

In November Lyons silk workers, alarmingly aided by National Guard units, rebelled against depressed wages and the Orleanists. Within a few hours revolutionaires controlled the second most important city of France. Louis Philippe sent Marshal Soult and nearly a tenth of the entire French army to recapture Lyons from the rebels. Soult and the king's son, the Duke of Orleans, forcibly entered the city on December 2, a date fraught with meaning.

Within the one year of 1831 anarchy had generated widespread and almost continuous riots as well as seven more distinct and disparate plots: four republican, two legitimist, and one Bonaparte. In 1832 insurrections featured diverse forces: ragpickers, the queen's niece, and two prominent generals. Meanwhile, cholera claimed thousands of Parisians (861 died on one day, April 9) and artillery wagons with stacked and swaying coffins unceremoniously picked up the bodies. Panicked Parisians fled in terror from the macabre convoys and ragpickers claimed that the government had poisoned water and wine to destroy the poorer classes. Casimir Périer, "created by God for a wild and excited period," suppressed disorder with a ferocity that terrified even his partisans.

The popular Duchess of Berry, niece of Louis Philippe's wife, landed near Marseille April 28, 1832, to claim the throne for her son, the Bourbon Count of Chambord, the Duke of Bordeaux, Henry V. This right wing insurgency broke out first in the Vendée. Although adherents collapsed rapidly, the elusive duchess led Louis Philippe's forces on a frustrating chase before she was apprehended over six months later.

Violent rioting broke out, allegedly with Lafayette's help, at General Lamarque's funeral on June 5. Lamarque, whom Napoleon had promoted to marshal at Saint-Helena, had been an active leader of the opposition party until cholera abruptly ended his life. When Bonapartists led mourners to salute the emperor's column in the Place Vendôme, tension mounted and, as the cortege moved on, the crowd began to sing the revolutionary *Marseillaise*. Shouts of "Vive la République" were followed with "Aux armes!" Shots rang out, the cavalry charged, barricades went up and, in the Tuileries, there was talk of flight. Only after eight hundred victims and two days of bitter fighting could the 40,000-man Paris garrison curb the insurrection.

A fortnight after Lamarque's tempestuous funeral, Prince Metternich announced that the Duke of Reichstadt would not live much longer, simultaneously alerting French officials to the danger of Louis Napoleon, the "acknowledged" Bonaparte successor and "a man tied up with plots." The Austrian foreign minister had perceptively foretold both events. Napoleon's twenty-one year old son died at Schonbrunn July 22, 1832 and Louis Napoleon, Italian revolutionary and nephew of the emperor, became the Bonaparte heir.

Relief and renewed problems followed. With any title—the King of Rome, the Duke of Reichstadt, Napoleon II, or l'Aiglon—the emperor's son had provided succor to Bonapartists and was used by Metternich as a potential threat to the restored monarchs of

France. The new heir, beyond the reach of Vienna and more gregarious than his younger cousin, lived closer to France, not far from the Franco-Swiss border. The emperor's sword, passed on to him, was ultimately to become a sceptre in his hands.

For Louis Philippe, however, assassination attempts in 1832 appeared more urgently threatening than Louis Napoleon. Despite article twelve of the Charter—"The person of the King is inviolable and sacred"—in November an assailant fired at Louis Philippe as he crossed a bridge. An empathetic jury incredibly acquitted the suspect "for lack of evidence." In the next three years there were to be seven more distinct plots and four attempted assassinations.

Orleanist foreign policy in 1833 invited tantalizing and unflattering comparison to Napoleon. French troops massed near the Spanish border but did not move when the September 29 death of Ferdinand VII initiated six years of Carlist civil war. At the opposite end of the Mediterranean, Russia and the sultan scorned Louis Philippe and opposed the forces of Mehemet Ali, a French ally and the emperor's protege. The Russo-Turkish treaty of Unkiar Skelessi (July 10, 1833) was distinctly an international public defeat for France.

In April of 1834, the Orleanists themselves believed a coup d'état could easily occur because of the army's discontent. Royal troops and artillerymen fought a bitter five-day battle, quelling a Parisian uprising and a second Lyons revolt. There were a thousand casualties and rioters were animated by bizarre rumors: Louis Philippe was dead, a republic had been established, and Lucien Bonaparte had been declared first consul. Regular troops and the National Guard crushed a two-day Parisian insurrection, led by the republican Rights of Man society. Surprisingly, however, the death of Lafayette in May aroused no outburst.

Nevertheless, the tribulations of Louis Philippe continued. An elaborate attempt to kill him in 1835 with an "infernal machine" (a primitive machine gun—twenty-five gun barrels bound together) resulted in the execution of two Parisian revolutionaries and a

Corsican, Joseph Fieschi, a former non-commissioned officer. This near-miss was to affect Louis Napoleon and also French foreign policy. The tsar's congratulatory note to Louis Philippe was diplomatically correct, although noticeably aloof; conspicuously, Nicholas I's condolence to the family of Mortier, Napoleon's marshal killed by Fieschi, was affectionately personal. Prince Metternich himself orchestrated concerted action from Vienna, Berlin, and St. Petersburg; all of the ministries expressed skepticism about the French king's longevity. The Austrian foreign minister took it upon himself to give "very precise instructions" if the king's luck—and life—expired.

Although Louis Philippe prudently began using an armored coach in late 1835, within six months the fortified vehicle revealed both its limitations and the king's unremitting vulnerability. A bullet from Alibaud's "cane-gun" barely missed him as he left the Louvre with his wife and sister on June 25, 1836. This prompted Talleyrand's niece, the Duchess of Dino, to irreverently quip, "That shot, I am afraid, has killed our Royal Princess." And so it did. The precarious position of the French king dashed impending marriage arrangements with Austrian Archduchess Theresa.

Contrasting embarrassingly with Napoleon's marriage to a Hapsburg princess, the Austrian court snubbed the Orleanist proposal to the daughter of Archduke Charles, so frequently defeated by Bonaparte he had become almost popular in France. The Duke of Orleans had gone to Vienna to propose in March of 1836, but despite jeweler Bapst's "diplomatic wonders"—snuff-boxes and portraits set in diamonds—Metternich protested, "It is impossible to expose an Austrian princess to driving in a carriage riddled every minute with pistol shots." Archduke Charles, equally brusque in spurning the French heir, announced, "My daughter does not feel strong enough to compete with the dangers to which the French royal family remains unhappily exposed." Chagrined, Louis Philippe next considered Marie of Baden, a Bonaparte princess and Louis Napoleon's cousin, as a prospective consort for his eldest son.

Thiers even suggested Mathilde Bonaparte, Jerome's daughter and another cousin of Louis Napoleon. Finally in 1837 the Duke of Orleans married Princess Helena of Mecklenburg-Schwerin.

Unrelenting attacks may have caused the allegation by Alexis de Tocqueville that Louis Philippe understood people only through their vices and his "only kingly virtue" seemed to be courage. This is somewhat understandable, given the provocations the monarch endured. Included in the many diabolically creative attempts on his life was a box of rattlesnakes (paralyzed by the cold and charily opened by the police) that arrived for the king from South America. The incessant fragility of the Orleanist monarch tempted assassins, complicated foreign relations, and encouraged further opposition. Louis Napoleon interpreted the disorders in France and the attempts on the monarch's life as obvious proof that the Orleanists were not well established. Bourbons had been largely discredited with the failure of the 1832 attempted restoration and, with the deaths of Lafayette in 1834 and Carrel in 1836, there were no significant republican leaders. Bonapartism seemed the obvious alternative.

• • •

As the Bonaparte heir, Louis Napoleon had to make himself more widely known. Banished from his homeland at age seven, to most Frenchmen in the 1830s he was simply one of Napoleon's many nephews. Throughout France in 1831 he had seen busts and portraits of his grandmother Josephine, his mother Hortense, and his uncles, particularly Napoleon and Eugene. Nevertheless, he deplored, "For the people, all the Bonapartes were dead." His complaint may have motivated his uncle Joseph, former King of Spain, to begin collecting signatures on an unsuccessful petition to the chamber of deputies to repeal the family's banishment. The young heir was still restive.

> How can you expect the French to remember us,
> when by our own act we have sought oblivion for
> fifteen years; when, these fifteen years every action

of every member of my family has been inspired by the fear of compromising himself, and by that alone; when they have avoided every occasion of displaying their persons, every means of publicly recalling their memories to the mind of the people?

Louis Napoleon was partially correct. Prior to 1830, information collected by the ministry of the interior on Bonaparte family activities revealed only a plethora of trivia, no substantial political activity. However, the July Revolution and the death of the Duke of Reichstadt activated both Louis Napoleon and the older Bonapartes. Balzac's Doctor Benassis asserted, "In my opinion a man who has conceived a political system ought . . . to seize power, and to put it into effect." Unlike the Bourbon Count of Chambord, who patiently stood ready to return whenever God provided the "propitious moment," Louis Napoleon agreed with Balzac's prose and methodically worked to achieve his destiny by prodding, rather than waiting for providence. As noted by A.L. Guérard, Louis Napoleon turned sentimental Napoleonism into practical Bonapartism.

Two months before the Duke of Reichstadt died, Louis Napoleon published *Political Reflections*, his own outline for the government he wanted to establish. Though supplemented in 1839 by *Napoleonic Ideas*, in 1832 this brief pamphlet stood second only to the declarations of Napoleon at St. Helena as basic ideology for the Legend. This initiative however only earned criticism from his father who chastised his son's "frenzied desire for fame." Lucien regarded his nephew's work as "rash expressions" which were wrong and foolish for keeping alive pretensions and fostering dated recollections.

The ideas in *Political Reflections* were ostensibly the objectives of the Strasbourg coup. Denigrating the government of Louis Philippe as unstable, Louis Napoleon espoused the principles of a republic fused with the practicality of an empire. "If the Rhine were a sea" France could, perhaps, establish a republic. Threatening neighbors, however, mitigated against this since France was not an insular power. "The day will come, and perhaps not long hence, when virtue will triumph over intrigue, when merit will be stronger than prejudice, when glory will crown liberty!" This would be achieved by uniting two popular parties—Bonapartists and republicans—and by expanding the franchise, the foundation of Louis Napoleon's new government. "There will be no distinction of rank or fortune: every citizen will share equally in the election of the deputies. There will no longer be aristocracy of birth or aristocracy of money—there will be only the aristocracy of merit. The only qualification for the franchise will be age." An emperor would implement the popular will and the government would be stable, "in harmony with the wants and wishes of the majority." Opposition, "which should always exist in a free State, shall be only like the discords of music which are in harmony with the whole." Publication of *Political Reflections* accomplished one of his major objectives: to establish himself in the public image as a politically astute Bonaparte.

He sent a copy to Chateaubriand (twice mentioned in his pamphlet), who had, in October of 1831, eloquently protested the laws against Bonapartes although he, himself, remained an adherent of the Bourbons. The renowned author wrote Louis Napoleon, "You know, Prince, that my young king is (in exile) in Scotland, and that so long as he lives there can be no other king of France." But if God (and, presumably, Frenchmen) rejected the Bourbons, and if France restored a republic and held an election, "then, Prince, there is no name that befits the glory of France better than yours." Before July 1832, Chateaubriand addressed Louis Napoleon as Count, thereafter he deferentially began using the title, Prince.

After the death of the Duke of Reichstadt, many distinguished guests made their way to Arenenberg to give homage to the new Bonaparte heir and, perhaps, to hedge against the quirks of politics. Involved with the Duchess of Berry's attempt against Louis Philippe, Chateaubriand initially apologized for being too busy for a trip to Switzerland. However, he adroitly found time for the journey after the Duke of Reichstadt's death, reaching Lake Constance on August 29, 1832, thirty-eight days after Louis Napoleon became the heir.

Other visitors making the pilgrimage to Arenenberg in August of 1832 included Alexandre Dumas, the famous author who had manned the barricades during the 1830 revolution, and Madame Julie de Récamier, a legitimist celebrated for her beauty, charm, and conversation in literary and political circles during the Empire. An avowed republican, Dumas divulged to Hortense the many divisions among republicans; he also admitted his ambivalence toward the Orleanist government. "I neither accept it or challenge it; I submit to it." Undoubtedly welcome news, Louis Napoleon's mother encouraged him to speak frankly of the Bonapartists. Although he revered the emperor, he told her the Duke of Reichstadt would have had no chance of success. Hortense revealingly protested. "What you say is not very consoling for those of his family who should preserve some hopes."

Despite Alexandre Dumas' pessimism, Louis Napoleon tenaciously pursued recognition and his goals. Early in 1833 he published a second study, *A Consideration of Swiss Politics and Military Affairs*. Starting out with a justification of Napoleon's political system, he went on to defend both the satellite kingdoms and his father's defiance of the emperor. "My father thought he could not unite the interests of the people he was called upon to govern with those of France, and he preferred to lose his throne sooner than act against his conscience or his brother. History rarely offers so fine an example of disinterested loyalty." Louis Napoleon argued that a republic, the government of several, would be susceptible to the tyranny of aristocrats. He pointed out the despotism of republics, particularly in Italy. "Venetian laws were written in blood." Although a good republic "is the best form of government, a tyrannical republic is the worst form, for it is easier to cast aside the yoke of one than that of several." Another example, all of the Swiss cantons were in a state of ferment. "The Swiss Confederation is a republic, but she is not free; she appears to govern herself, but it is the spirit of the Holy Alliance that directs her." Once more alluding to the vulnerability of Louis Philippe, Louis Napoleon added, "Stability alone makes the happiness of a people." France is preoccupied with "fear of an approaching disturbance."

Although this publication earned him considerable respect in Switzerland, its major appeal lay in its allusions to the Empire. In 1834 the canton of Berne made him a captain of artillery in the Swiss army and, to acknowledge this honor, he produced yet another book, an impressive five-hundred-page *Swiss Artillery Manual,* dedicated to the officers of the Ecole d'Application at Thun as "a remembrance of the time we have spent together." As a Bonaparte this artillery work considerably enhanced his credentials among French officers. That year on August 15, the emperor's birthday, a dinner attended by major garrison officers quickly became an occasion for enthusiastic toasts to Louis Napoleon. He had now gained real recognition as a professional military figure, a key ingredient in his status as a Bonaparte pretender.

Strasbourg in 1836

RUE DU FAUBOURG DE PIERRE

FINKMATT BARRACKS

RUE GRAUMANN

PLACE D'ARMES

HOTEL DE VILLE

JEWISH QUARTER

N

ILL RIVIERE

PONT NEUF

AUSTERLITZ BARRACKS

PLACE ST. NICOLAS

RUE DES ORPHELINS

ARSENAL

(Based primarily on J.N. Villot's 1842 map)

CITADEL

Chapter Four

The General Plan

By the end of 1835 Louis Napoleon had clearly established himself as the bona fide Bonaparte pretender to the throne of France. He saw the nation as seething with pro-Napoleonic sentiment but saddled with an unpopular regime. Despite the failure of a variety of conspiracies and plots against the Orleans government, he felt that if the public could be properly mobilized, Louis Philippe would fall and a Bonaparte could once again rule in France. However, it would take some sort of dramatic event of Napoleonic proportions; and in his uncle's Return from Elba, Louis believed that history had provided him with the key to his destiny.

Napoleon Bonaparte's life had been littered with extraordinary episodes, but few captured the age's romantic imagination more than his Return from Elba in 1815. The escape from his island prison, the march on Paris despite forces sent to capture him, and the overthrow of the restored Bourbon regime – all with neither bloodshed nor a shot being fired – were unparalleled in political history. It was as dramatic and daring as any of his finest triumphs. Further, the weakness of a regime based on foreign bayonets in defiance of popular feeling could hardly have been more glaringly illustrated.

As Louis Napoleon pondered his uncle's return to power in 1815, a vague blueprint took shape in his mind, a procedure by which he could overthrow Louis Philippe. He should appear with at least a modest force at some point on the border of France, invoke the memory of Napoleon and the Empire, and then march on Paris, attracting enthusiastic recruits along the way. For him, the events of 1815 proved that such a course of action could be both bloodless and unstoppable.

This view of Napoleon's return ignored a few realities. After the emperor had landed at Golfe Juan near Cannes, a portion of his 1100 man force had been quickly captured. Also, the route of the march to Paris had carefully avoided areas known to be sympathetic to the Bourbons. Thus, his triumphal march was not exactly the same as an overwhelming referendum. Unlike his nephew, however, Napoleon was able to start his adventure with a small force already in hand, but had the special challenge of having to transport it secretly from Elba to France.

To Louis Napoleon the main outlines to be followed seemed clear and adjustments to his particular situation could easily be made. Lacking any vestige of a real armed force, he believed he could acquire one by winning over a frontier garrison. This would provide him far more military strength than his uncle had had and from there, the rest of the plan would readily unfold. The primary question then became, where? Once this was decided, detailed planning could take place to win over the specific garrison. There was no question in his mind that, given a proper occasion, the army would desert the Orleanists to support a Napoleonic restoration. It had after all deserted the Bourbons in favor of the Orleanists and in the army the Legend was particularly strong. Unlike republicans who wanted to weaken the army, Louis Napoleon's intent was to enlist the military in his coup. While specific units of a garrison were being mobilized for his cause, he reasoned that the area's citizenry, properly placarded and similarly imbued with the Legend, would also join the enthusiasm generated for his coup. All this he expected to accomplish simply on the strength of the name "Napoleon". While he judged winning military adherents as an essential first step, he was emphatic that there should be no bloodshed. He did not contemplate a military overthrow of the government but simply an energizing and mobilizing of what he believed

was a latent smouldering national will. As he reviewed various pos-
sibilities, the Strasbourg garrison emerged more and more as a likely place for a successful coup.

Strasbourg had a general record of instability, as well as special
indications of outright disloyalty. Republican and anti-government
activity, especially among non-commissioned officers and in the
artillery, had increased markedly in the early 1830s. According to
the minister of the interior in 1835, the army had "a mass of ardent
young men who dream of the heroic follies of the Empire". Low
pay, inadequate pensions, and the slow promotion rates of peace-
time, all supplemented by government instability, fostered insubordination, indiscipline and even disloyalty. An 1836 inspection
report noted ominously that for two years there had been no promotions among artillery non-commissioned officers, a group
"whose support is so essential for the government and whose influence on the troops was so convincingly demonstrated in the 1830
revolution". At that time Strasbourg artillery officers had drawn up
an indictment of Charles X and pressured all but two of their colleagues to sign it. Many artillery men at Strasbourg had deserted
their posts, going to Paris to participate in the revolution. By 1832
over half of all French officers had been drawn from the disgruntled
non-commissioned ranks and among the senior officers a large
number were veterans of the Empire. A further consideration was
that in 1836 the Strasbourg garrison included Napoleon's old regiment, the 4th artillery, which had played a major role in his libera-
tion of Toulon in 1793 and had also opened the gates of Grenoble
to him on the seventh of the Hundred Days in March of 1815.
Louis Napoleon believed that such groups would obviously be susceptible to an appeal for support of a program headed by a
Bonaparte and promising a regime based on patriotism and respect
for military glory. An added pledge of universal suffrage would
attract republicans, a strongly militant segment of the Strasbourg
populace as well as within its garrison. Almost an incidental advantage was that the former Grand Duchess of Baden, Stephanie de

Beauharnais, a third cousin of Louis Napoleon, resided at Freiburg, near Strasbourg, thus providing a protected haven where interviews could easily be held with members of the garrison. Strasbourg appeared indeed a promising setting for a successful coup.

Meanwhile Franco-Swiss relations were, at best, uneasy. Adolphe Thiers' government suspected that the Swiss were harboring exiles involved in subversive plots against Louis Philippe. This apprehension led to Paris sending spies into Switzerland to acquire information on suspected plotters, including Louis Napoleon. In Berne the French ambassador supervising these agents happened to be a man who had been baptized with Louis Napoleon, the Duke of Montebello, a son of Marshal Lannes. When Louis was in Baden, the prefect at Strasbourg, Augustin Choppin-d'Arnouville also had him watched. All of these efforts, however, were clumsy, amateurish and ill-conceived.

In July, 1836, acting on orders from Paris, Montebello began to pressure the reluctant Swiss government to arrest and expel one Auguste Conseil, an alleged anti-French revolutionary. The name on his phony passport was Napoleon Cheli, contrived to appear both Bonapartist and Corsican. He also had a second alias, François Hermann. The upshot of the episode was that Conseil proved in reality to be a French agent, selected specifically by Louis Philippe and sent to Switzerland to report on subversives and to contrive a plot serious enough to justify a French intervention. Actually, Montebello knew the truth of his mission but went along with his instructions, thinking they were to reinforce Conseil's cover as a genuine republican. When the truth came out, ministers in Paris were appalled and belatedly the minister of the interior, Montalivet, assumed responsibility for Conseil's mission. However, the damage had been done, the ministers were embarrassed and France humiliated, while the Swiss assumed a posture of righteous indignation.

The efforts to report on Louis Napoleon while he was in Baden were hardly more impressive. Choppin-d'Arnouville assured the commandant at Strasbourg that "I have an agent near him and he takes no step of which I am not informed." This confident assertion however was considerably weakened when he also noted that his police spy was a "common officer" who lacked enough social standing to infiltrate the prince's society and, accordingly, could only observe Louis Napoleon in public places. Could Choppin-d'Arnouville have been deliberately inept? The prefect was regarded as an effective administrator, his career stretching back to the Empire; but the extent of his diligence in hiring a proper agent on this occasion is certainly subject to question, particularly when, with the wisdom of hindsight, we know that he later served on several missions for Louis Napoleon after he became the Emperor Napoleon III. Thus inadequate spies, superficial sleuthing, lack of ministerial coordination and ignored reports – all exposed a simplistic and humiliating clumsiness on the part of Louis Philippe's government.

After Louis Napoleon had become the recognized Bonaparte pretender, the volume and variety of visitors to Arenenberg increased markedly. In addition to the usual old soldiers and officials from the Empire, Bonaparte and Beauharnais relatives, Chateaubriand, Alexandre Dumas, Marshal Marmont's estranged wife, the Duchess of Ragusa, Madame de Récamier and Madame LeHon, now the guests also included the Duchess de Dino, Talleyrand's niece, sent from London by the wily diplomat to make an assessment of the young prince. Since accommodations at Arenenberg were quite limited, many visitors stayed at nearby Wolfsberg, "an establishment half-chateau, half-boarding house", owned by an old friend and veteran of the Empire, Charles Denis Parquin.

"Old friend and veteran of the Empire" hardly does justice to the part played by Parquin in the life of Louis Napoleon. Parquin had met Louis' father in 1805 at a regimental review in Paris. The next year as King of Holland, Louis again reviewed Parquin's regiment. At the same time Parquin also saw Queen Hortense in a carriage accompanied by her companion, Louise Cochelet. Though instantly attracted to Louise, he did not see her again until fifteen years later, in July 1821, when the two were in a coach from Switzerland to Paris. The next year Charles and Louise were married in the small chapel at Arenenberg, with the former Viceroy of Italy, Prince Eugene de Beauharnais, serving as a witness to the ceremony. A daughter, Claire, was born a year later. In 1824 the Parquins purchased Wolfsberg (actually Louise bought it) and the couple settled into a community rife with other aging veterans of the Empire, all regular visitors at Arenenberg.

Although Parquin was nearly twenty-two years older than Louis, the two became fast friends. The regular appearance of Parquin in Louis Napoleon's life in the 1820s was providential. For years the veteran soldier waxed eloquently to the impressionable teenager about episodes from his career between 1803 and 1815. Parquin's stories of martial heroism were a graphic dimension of the Empire, combining neatly with Hortense's steady indoctrination of her son in the Legend. In this heady atmosphere they discussed the Empire, current problems in France and the chances for some sort of eventual Bonaparte restoration.

Charles Parquin had been raised in a bourgeois family which had little regard for the military. When he enlisted at sixteen in the 20th chasseurs (cavalry), neither of his parents approved. His mother viewed the army as simply a "career for idlers". His first direct encounter with the violence of warfare came at Jena, October 14, 1806. While standing beside his regiment's commander, Colonel Marigny, a cannonball decapitated Marigny. Under the general command of Murat, Parquin's regiment then helped to drive the Prussians to the Baltic, a pursuit causing Napoleon to remark, "After Jena, the light cavalry capitalized the victory all on its own." At Eylau on February 8, 1807, Parquin's 20th chasseurs received both heavy losses from the Russians but further accolades from the emperor who watched the battle.

A week later Parquin and fifty of his advanced guard were moving toward Konigsberg where they were captured by the Russians in the village of Trunkestein. Cossack lance-thrusts slashed Parquin five times after his dead horse had pinned him down. In severe pain and cold, he joined two hundred fifty other French prisoners in Vilna. From there they painfully walked to Vladimir, northeast of Moscow, en route to Siberia. At Vladimir news arrived of the treaty of Tilsit, and Parquin retraced grueling steps back across Russia, joining his regiment at Stolp, northeast of Berlin, on October 15, 1807. Severely wounded again at Amstettin, Parquin and his brigade were prominent in the victory at Wagram. Serving in the Iberian Peninsula from July, 1810 to October, 1812, he received more wounds and a testimony to his valor signed by Marshal Marmont. Returning to Paris he stepped down in rank to become a lieutenant in the Old Guard's chasseur regiment. He received the coveted Cross of the Legion of Honor and on April 10, 1813 left France to join the Army of Germany, then under the personal command of the emperor. At Leipzig he saved the life of a grateful Marshal Oudinot. He sustained a bayonet wound directly across his face during battle at Hanau, October 30, 1813, and six weeks later he became a captain in the Imperial Guard's second regiment. On a special mission ordered personally by Napoleon during the dramatic defensive campaign of 1814, Parquin captured a hundred Russian and Prussian prisoners. Leading a charge against the Russians two weeks later, he captured eighteen cannon and nearly six hundred prisoners. Of this latter event, General Sebastiani remarked to Napoleon, "I have been a cavalry officer for twenty-five years and do not ever remember seeing a more brilliant charge." In this last battle of the Guard, the emperor himself, sword in hand at the head of the Guard's cavalry, followed up Parquin's charge and pursued the fleeing Russians. A month later Parquin stood with the Guard at Fontainebleu and listened to Napoleon's famous farewell. He remained in the army until January 1, 1824.

1820 had been a year of plots against the established order and investigations uncovered a conspiracy within the army. While Parquin was not directly involved, when he refused to denounce participants, he was himself discharged. Later he often casually referred to his career as "eleven campaigns, eleven wounds" but this modesty hardly reflected the fact that he had testimonials to his courage and ability from two marshals, had earned the Cross of the Legion of Honor and personal praise from the emperor. Dumas characterized him as "one of those men of the empire who are entirely devoted to the imperial tradition" and it is little wonder that episodes from his career made indelible impressions on the young Louis Napoleon.

After the revolution which had brought him to power, Louis Philippe made a number of conciliatory gestures to various elements whom the Bourbons had alienated. Among those were ordinances of August 28 and September 18, 1830, reserving half of officer vacancies for imperial veterans and also reinstating with full seniority those who had been retired on half-pay. Although Parquin scorned the political outcome of the 1830 revolution, Hortense advised him to accept the opportunity to resume his career. Accordingly, in late 1830, Parquin was appointed a gendarmerie squadron commander of the Department of the Lower Rhine. While residing at Strasbourg with his wife and child, he learned of Louis Napoleon's involvement in the Italian revolution, exploits in which he appears to have been in no way involved. In the next summer he was named the gendarmerie commandant at Doubs and moved to Basançon. After only a brief stay, he requested and received an indefinite leave, returning to Wolfsberg just as Louis and Hortense were arriving home from England. As a seasoned veteran, Parquin had regarded himself as above gendarmerie duty and his wife had been unhappy in Besançon. After the death of the Duke of Reichstadt made Louis the recognized imperial pretender, Parquin went to London in 1832 and participated in the Bonaparte family conference. This trip was certainly far beyond what would be expected from a neighbor or even a very close friend. At this point he was clearly a trusted confidante regarding intimate Bonaparte strategy. He left England in February 1833, about three months before Louis. When Louis returned to Arenenberg, Parquin dramatically met him in uniform, announcing himself as a "Soldat de l'Empéreur!"

Up to 1835 Parquin was clearly Louis Napoleon's closest confidante and the first recruit for any coup attempt. Between February and May of 1835, however, his interests became preoccupied by the illness and death of his wife. He had a daughter to care for and little money; but the Grand Duchess Stephanie came to his rescue, taking twelve year old Claire to be educated at a Mannheim convent. Now alone, Parquin again turned to the only profession he knew, the army. In December of 1835 a royal ordinance named him a lieutenant colonel and battalion head in the Paris Municipal Guard, forerunner of the present Republican Guard. Six months later he was back at Arenenberg on a regular leave prepared to settle his wife's affairs and to sell Wolfsberg.

In 1835 while Parquin was consumed with his family crisis, his influence at Arenenberg was somewhat superceded by the appearance of another dedicated Bonapartist. This was Jean Gilbert Victor Fialin, the son of a tax collector, a bright and aggressive social climber with pretensions of aristocracy, calling himself the Viscount de Persigny. The same age as Louis Napoleon, he had spent two years at the cavalry school at Saumur. Leaving there in 1828, he was assigned to a regiment of hussars (light cavalry) as sergeant major. Here he was exposed to republican ideas which he readily and openly espoused. After the 1830 revolution his blunt republican remarks led to his dismissal from the army for insubordination. His republicanism had bred a disaffection for the Bourbon regime and now he was similarly estranged from the government of Louis Philippe.

After leaving the army Persigny tried his hand at journalism. While traveling in Baden, a chance event occurred which he claimed changed the whole direction of his life. His driver shouted, "Vive Napoléon!" to the occupant of a passing carriage and explained to Persigny that this was Louis Napoleon, the son of Louis and Hortense, the former monarchs of Holland. Actually, the other traveler was not Louis but one of his cousins. However, Persigny saw this trivial incident as a mystical, almost religious experience; and at once he became an avid convert to Bonapartism. He now read voraciously about Napoleon and the Empire, even started a Bonapartist journal, and talked incessantly about the Empire and prospects for its restoration with any who would listen. Many described him as more Bonapartist than the Bonapartes. While Parquin was essentially a soldier, Persigny was a conspirator. Although driven by a romantic emotionalism, his mind was incisive. Becoming acquainted with ex-Kings Joseph and Jerome, he appeared at Arenenberg in June of 1835 with a letter of introduction to Louis Napoleon. Arriving as Parquin was absorbed with his family problems, Persigny at once became a central figure in the planning of a coup at Strasbourg. To the heady mystical forces swirling about Louis Napoleon and in his character, Persigny brought even more emotional commitment but a dose of practicality as well. The general idea of a coup thus began to take more concrete form.

Chapter Five

Personnel And Preparations

The next year, from mid 1835 to mid 1836, was given over to attention to specific details. Parquin was left out of this phase and must have felt shunted aside by his young protégée. His friend of fourteen years had found another confidante his own age and conversations which the old soldier attended now at Arenenberg were less serious and about topics other than a coup.

The period of background planning and recruiting involved trips by Persigny to Paris and various points in eastern France, including Strasbourg. Louis Napoleon also visited sites in eastern France as well as Baden and locations in Switzerland. Both men used assumed names in their efforts to discover potential supporters, and in political correspondence the prince frequently made use of code words, a practice he had learned years before from Hortense. To her Bonapartes were "Nuzillards", republicans "Barillots", Bourbons "Bassards" and Orleanists were "Metrots".

Persigny believed Bonapartism to be essentially a matter of simple patriotism and above the level of mere political parties. He had no hesitation in approaching anyone who might be a prospect, no matter what their known political leanings. Thus, for example, the legitimist Viscount Frédéric de Falloux twice declined Persigny's invitations to join the cause of Louis Napoleon but ruefully conceded later that "at this time of my life, an air of adventure did not displease me". He was an example of many prominent figures who, knowing that plans for a coup were afoot, declined an offer to participate and yet failed to inform anyone in the government.

Between them, Louis Napoleon and Persigny were able to find enough sympathizers that they felt justified in proceeding with their plans, but they encountered frustrations as well. None of the feelers extended to general officers were successful; and Louis reluctantly concluded that while their assistance would have been helpful, it was not essential.

The biggest disappointment was the failure of efforts to recruit fifty-five year old Lieutenant General Theophile Voirol, Strasbourg's garrison commander. Under the Empire he had ably commanded the 8th infantry regiment and had rallied to Napoleon during the Hundred Days. Forced out of the military in 1816 for "a politically reprehensible attitude", he was reinstated in 1819 as colonel of the Basses-Pyrenees department legion and promoted to marechal de camp (brigadier general) in 1823. Ten years later he was a lieutenant general and second in command of the Army of Africa from April 1833 to July 1834. Transferred from Algeria he was named head of the 5th military division at Strasbourg on December 21, 1835. After only seven months in his new post, an "agent" of Louis Napoleon, probably Persigny, conveyed to him a letter from the Bonaparte prince, asking for a meeting. Voirol greeted this approach with a gruff refusal and specifically refused the prince access to Strasbourg. However, since Voirol was known to recall fondly his service during the Empire and three months earlier had even sent Hortense a gift of perfume, Louis Napoleon decided that despite the general's strong sense of duty, he, like a number of others, should be regarded as a cautious sympathizer, one who might support a Bonapartist coup once such an event got underway.

Louis Napoleon's plans for the Strasbourg garrison were particularly disturbing for another officer. Aimé François Thierry de Franqueville had been a captain in 1814 and led a battalion during the Hundred Days. In 1836 at age forty-eight, he was a commandant at Strasbourg and General Voirol's aide-de-camp. At the time Voirol sent Hortense perfume, Franqueville had also sent her a purse. Imbued with a strong sense of duty and loyalty to Voirol, his strong feelings for the Bonapartes rendered his position precarious. It was further complicated by an interesting additional circumstance. His wife was Laure Masuyer, daughter of Gabriel Masuyer, a liberal professor at Strasbourg's School of Medicine. She had two sisters, both close to the Bonapartes: Fanny was companion to Louis Napoleon's cousin Stephanie; and Valerie, a companion to Hortense. Valerie's godmother was the Empress Josephine and on January 6, 1810 she had met Napoleon at Malmaison. Letters passed freely between the sisters and in visits back and forth they served as couriers. Laure had conveyed the purse and perfume to Hortense along with some correspondence, including communications between Louis Napoleon and various officers of the Strasbourg garrison . The sisters in fact played an important role in the developing plot, and Valerie's memoirs are an interesting source for this period in Louis Napoleon's life. Franqueville proved unable to remain as aloof from the gathering crisis as his commander, as late as August of 1836 having "interests to take care of for the prince". Laure curiously believed that Parquin was the major instigator of their dilemma, referring to the colonel as "that miserable Parquin".

General Voirol's overtly unequivocal rebuff to Louis Napoleon was not mirrored by his direct subordinate, Colonel Claude Nicholas Vaudrey, a graduate of the Ecole Polytechnique and a most important convert to Louis Napoleon. At fifty-two years of age he was the second in command of the garrison, in charge of all the artillery and the direct commanding officer of the 4th artillery regiment. Highly esteemed, his contemporaries described him in superlative terms: distinguished, tall and impressive, aristocratic, determined, pragmatic, educated, fastidiously groomed, with a military bearing enhancing a refined sophistication and quiet strength. That he commanded the 4th artillery with all its evocations of glory made him a very special adherent.

Vaudrey's career during the Empire had been outstanding.

Enlisting in 1804 at the age of twenty, he fought in major campaigns between 1806 and 1815, save for 1814 when he was a prisoner of war. In 1813 the emperor personally promoted him on the field of battle when he was covered with wounds. At Waterloo he commanded a battery of eighteen guns and again received multiple wounds. His bravery was beyond question and had earned him an officer's rank in the Legion of Honor.

Despite Vaudrey's eleven years of service to France and Napoleon, the Bourbon government of Louis XVIII banned him and thousands of others from the army. When Charles X came to the throne, he was able to resume his career in 1826 and was at Strasbourg in 1830 during that year's unrest. Promoted to colonel in September 1830, he was given command of the 4th artillery on May 28, 1833. Since 1815 slow promotions had been a recognized problem, especially in the artillery where officers had virtually no chance to distinguish themselves. An army reorganization of March 9, 1834, had even slowed the process, particularly irritating career soldiers. For an officer who had received three of his promotions within six years during the Empire, it was discouraging. Vaudrey twice requested assignment as aide-de-camp to the Duke of Orleans and twice his application was denied. Subsequent allegations, however, that he joined Louis Napoleon because of dissatisfaction with his rank appear to be unjustified. He was, after all, the second in command at Strasbourg, the ranking artillery officer, had been promoted, given command of the 4th, and by October of 1836 anticipated promotion to marechal de camp, a major career step.

In early 1836 Vaudrey received a letter from Louis Napoleon, enclosed with a copy of the *Swiss Artillery Manual*. Seeking Bonaparte sympathizers who were disillusioned with the Orleanists, the prince had similarly contacted many French officers. The colonel decided to respond and an exchange of correspondence followed. Using the name of Louise Wernert (or Vernert), Louis Napoleon referred to the planned coup in his letters as the "marriage" of Louise Wernert. By late April 1836 Vaudrey decided to meet with this nephew of his revered and romanticized emperor. Some have credited Parquin with arranging for the two to meet, but Persigny also had contacts in Strasbourg and could have served in this role. In any event, in late July 1836, Vaudrey and Louis Napoleon met for the first time in Baden, introduced by a retired artillery officer, Colonel Eggerle. On this occasion the idea of a coup at Strasbourg was openly discussed and after a number of initial objections, Vaudrey endorsed the general plan. Later he was to raise further questions, causing some historians to suggest that he only formally adhered to the plot as late as October, but Vaudrey himself testified that it was on this occasion at Baden that he had been won over by Louis Napoleon.

The adhesion of Colonel Vaudrey provided Louis with a solid foothold within Strasbourg. The major portion of the 10,000 man garrison then quartered in the city was comprised of three infantry regiments (the 14th, 16th and 46th), two artillery regiments (the 3rd and 4th) and an engineering battalion of pontonniers (bridge builders). Virtually all these units had been regularly reported for unrest and republican activity. Local republicans supported Bonapartist opposition to the Orleans regime and the 4th artillery had actually harbored a secret society in 1833. The next year six of its officers had been arrested for political activity. It was a garrison rife with Bonapartist sentiment and Louis Napoleon had ample reason to believe it might readily follow an appeal to overthrow the regime in Paris.

Another officer from the garrison joining the conspiracy in July of 1836 was Lieutenant François Armand Laity. A twenty-four year old graduate of the Ecole Polytechnique, he was an artillery officer assigned to the pontonnier battalion. This unit had been at Strasbourg since 1818, and as the inspector general of artillery, General Lenoury, observed in 1834, had been infected by excessive exposure to the area's subversive political values. Laity was to prove an especially important recruit. Also joining the plot was twenty-seven year old Major Jules Barthélemy Lombard, a military surgeon at Strasbourg with strong Bonapartist leanings and a record of opposition to Louis Philippe. Other officers within the garrison were also to support the coming coup, but most of them joined later and were not early participants in the planning.

At the Baden meeting Vaudrey had pointed out that the support of one regiment such as the 4th artillery was not enough to ensure success; but Louis Napoleon explained that he believed he would also attract support throughout the garrison and especially among non-commissioned officers, a judgment that was to prove sound. His cause was also adopted by several officers of the 3rd artillery and, outside of Strasbourg, by officers in the 3rd cuirassiers at Haguenau, the 6th cuirassiers at New Breisach, and the 7th light infantry at Nancy.

An interesting infantry recruit from Nancy was twenty-five year old Lieutenant Henri-Richard Alexander Siegfroi, the Viscount de Querelles. Arguing that "it is not necessary to have served the Emperor to admire his memory", he believed that the widespread discontent in the army would be a major factor in gaining adherents for a coup. Some accounts credit Persigny with recruiting him and indeed Persigny had written him, signing himself "Desrousseaux". Querelles, however, indicated that it had been the legitimist Count Raphael de Gricourt in 1836 who told him of a coup being planned and he had "instantly accepted" an invitation to join.

Imbued with the Legend and especially the Return from Elba, Querelles insisted at Strasbourg on carrying a banner surmounted by a silver imperial eagle which had belonged to the 7th infantry. He did this despite knowing that for such an action at Grenoble in 1815 Charles de la Bedoyer, a cousin of Hortense's lover, Flahaut, had been subsequently arrested, tried and shot, at age twenty nine. In 1841, Querelles was to marry a second cousin of Louis Napoleon, Countess Hermine Louise Françoise de Beauharnais who, after his death in 1848, wed Lieutenant Armand Laity, the conspirator already mentioned.

Raphael de Gricourt was associated with the coup at least as early as 1835, when he and Persigny were in London. While at the French hotel Grillon, he introduced Persigny to Falloux, an acquaintance from Paris who happened also to be a guest at the hotel. Persigny at once invited Falloux to join the plot. Though Falloux declined, this chance meeting proved to be the start of a lifelong friendship.

The twenty-three year old Gricourt was small, elegantly frail, and hardly looked the part of a conspirator. However, he hated the regime of Louis Philippe, had been arrested in 1832 for inciting the garrison at Quimper to revolt, and in 1836 was at Parquin's Wolfsberg chateau, frequently visiting at Arenenberg. Through the de Giacs he was related to the Beauharnais family and it had been his grandmother who had sold Saint Leu to Louis Bonaparte before he became the King of Holland. He also just happened to have an apartment in Strasbourg in the Rue Brulée.

Among the conspirators was a "rare beauty", Eleonore Gordon. Born in Paris just five months after Louis Napoleon, Eleonore Marie Brault was the daughter of a captain in the Imperial Guard and raised with a sense of Napoleonic loyalty. Educated first in a convent, she then studied music in conservatories in Paris and Milan. Talented and beautiful, at twenty-three she made her singing debut in Paris and went on to successful concerts in major continental cities. For a few years she was married to Sir Gordon-Archer, an English commissariat officer who perished from typhus while serving with the Anglo-Spanish legion.

Accounts of her life in the early 1830s differ widely. She was rich, she was poor, she was beautiful, she had been stabbed "full in the face" by an assailant. Testimony is similarly contradictory about when and how she met Louis Napoleon, Persigny and Vaudrey. According to a recent historian, Castelot, she was an ardent Bonapartist and because of Persigny's friendship with Louis Napoleon, fell into his arms the very first night she met him in London. Maybe, maybe not. She has even been confused with the

fictitious "Louise Wernert", Louis Napoleon's pseudonym in correspondence to Vaudrey.

She met Vaudrey on June 20, 1836 at a private concert which
she gave for General Voirol. Shortly thereafter she and Vaudrey
began an affair which was well underway by late July. After giving a
successful concert at the Reunion des Arts in Strasbourg on July 27,
she and Vaudrey went to Baden to meet Louis Napoleon. Some
accounts have suggested that she was "the decisive element" in winning over Vaudrey to the coup; but however appealing she may have
been, he had become interested in Louis Napoleon's prospects well
before meeting her.

Perhaps the least committed of the conspirators was Lieutenant
Colonel Frédéric Count de Bruc. Beginning his military career as a
teenager, in Napoleon's army he served as a major in the 4th chasseurs and an officer of the Legion of Honor. In 1830 he retired from
the army citing health reasons. His family was particularly prominent. His brother, the Marquis de Bruc de Malestroit, had married
Mlle. de Brissac, daughter of a peer of France and he himself had
served as a Gentleman of the Chamber for Charles X. Despite this
Bourbon connection and known from youth to have had an antipa-
thy towards Napoleon, he was related to the Beauharnais family and
now was a trusted friend of the Bonapartes and a visitor at
Arenenberg. De Bruc's family was reputed to be one of the wealth-
iest in France and his own assets "considerable". Nonetheless, he
claimed to be financially harassed by creditors, assuming pseudo-
nyms to avoid them, often calling himself the Count de Montaigu
after the name of his chateau or sometimes simply M. Bayard. He
demanded and received from Persigny 4500 francs for his support,
or at least his expenses, giving rise to the later allegation that he
alone of the plotters had adhered to the scheme for money. Later
General Pelletier was to point out that two officers involved in the
Strasbourg coup were indebted (Querelles and maybe Parquin) and
indeed that most officers involved in conspiracies since the
Restoration had "debts they could not have avoided". De Bruc's

financial difficulties may perhaps have been a matter of cash flow for he was a man with entrepreneurial instincts. One of his schemes was a colonization project for Algeria to include 30,000 volunteers for whom he would serve as commander for a three year period. Expenses would be 2,160,000 francs a year with fixed interest loans at 25% for the first year. The plan would profit investors but also help develop North Africa. He claimed the 4500 francs was Persigny's investment in the conquest of Tripoli. Considering the magnitude of de Bruc's plans, it seems unrealistic that he could be bought off for a sum of 4500 francs.

• • •

In July and August of 1836 the pace of preparations markedly increased. Most of these two months Louis spent in Baden meeting various supporters and spending all of his yearly allowance from his father. Also at this time Hortense sold some of her jewelry, suggesting that she may well have known of what was afoot. Just how much she knew of what was taking place has been one of the enduring peripheral questions regarding the conspiracy. Concurrent with this activity were arrangements being made for the young prince to marry his cousin, Mathilde, the daughter of Jerome, the ex-King of Westphalia. These were to fall through – the only marriage to take place being that of "Louise Wernert" at Strasbourg.

In July, 1836, Valerie Masuyer wrote her family in Strasbourg that Louis Napoleon would be passing through Offenbourg, southwest of Baden, and asked them to entertain him there. Since Offenbourg was the Masuyer family home, they dutifully made plans to comply. When Franqueville mentioned the coming meeting to a subordinate, Captain Alphonse Raindre, who was an admirer of Napoleon and curious about Louis Napoleon, the captain asked to be included. Along with Franqueville and his wife, Laure, he was cordially received and found himself impressed with the nephew of Napoleon.

At Offenbourg there was no mention of a conspiracy; but shortly thereafter Raindre received a letter from the prince suggesting a meeting on August 7 at a tavern in Kehl, near Strasbourg but across the Rhine. At the appointed time Louis Napoleon appeared, possibly with Persigny. He appeared ill, his eyes partially covered by a handkerchief. Raindre was taken aback and disillusioned. Louis came directly to the point, "Captain, you have courage and loyalty and I believe I can confide in you. You are as devoted to the Emperor as his family. An event is about to occur. I have counted on you and I am going to lead it".

Raindre later recalled that he expressed surprise about the plan and this seemed to irritate Louis Napoleon who replied, "I agree that it is novel, but we have methods to carry it out." Raindre claimed that he tried to dissuade him "for which he seemed to be grateful ....I told him he was unknown in France, that the Emperor's family was even more unknown perhaps than the Bourbons had been in 1814." At the end of the discussion Raindre promised not to divulge the meetings substance, but there can be no question whatever that he clearly understood that Louis Napoleon's plans "counted on the Strasbourg garrison."

Within a week, Raindre had second thoughts, Although Louis Napoleon had not revealed a specific date, the captain believed the coup would be attempted on August 15, the emperor's birthday. For two days he was "disturbed" and finally discussed his feelings with Franqueville who promised to keep the conversations secret unless necessity dictated otherwise. Some days later Raindre left for duty at New Breisach.

A week after Louis Napoleon's meeting with Raindre, Voirol received Louis Napoleon's letter vainly requesting a meeting. Voirol showed this to his aide-de-camp, Franqueville, who then divulged Raindre's contacts with Louis Napoleon. Voirol instructed Franqueville to deliver a verbal rebuff to Raindre but tempered the order by remarking, "I honour the memory of the Emperor, I respect and pity the misfortunes of his family."

Despite the rebuff from General Voirol, Louis Napoleon crossed the Rhine, probably on August 16, and entered Strasbourg.

Accompanied only by Persigny, he met about twenty-five officers who assured him, "The nephew of the Emperor is welcome. He has nothing to fear. He is under the protection of French honor. We would defend him at the price of our lives." Ironically, Captain Raindre was one of the officers at this meeting. Louis Napoleon briefly addressed the men and specifically wanted to know "whether I have deceived myself as to the sentiments of the army." All encouraged him and he left on August 18, convinced of solid support and utterly unaware that on the same day Voirol was communicating his plans to Paris.

On August 18 Voirol had become uneasy over the "gravity" of the situation and confronted his subordinate, Colonel Vaudrey, about contacts with the prince. Dissatisfied with Vaudrey's denials, he forwarded to Marshal Nicholas Joseph Maison, the minister of war, the letter he had received from Louis Napoleon as well as information about Louis Napoleon's contacts with garrison officers and Raindre's belief that a forceful coup was imminent. "The knowledge of this grave circumstance sufficiently explained to my mind the result the Prince had in mind asking to see me. Nothing less than the certainty of this would have determined me to trouble you with this affair." Having alerted the ministry in Paris, he apparently saw no need to inform the prefect, Choppin-d'Arnouville. Marshal Maison advised Voirol to redouble surveillance, especially in the case of granting permission for officers to visit Baden. However, less than three weeks later, on September 6, 1836, the ministry changed; and General Bernard, Louis Philippe's aide-de-camp, replaced Marshal Maison as the minister of war. It is not clear whether Maison ever informed others in the ministry of Voirol's letter.

By mid-August 1836, Louis Napoleon made the decision to attempt the coup in October. Returning to Arenenberg in late August, he found Parquin preparing to return to his post. He had settled most of his affairs and his leave was expiring. Financial uncertainties clouded his future and it was an unsettling time in his life. His wife had died, his daughter was in Baden and he had decided to sell Wolfsberg. This had been the only real home he had known in his adult life and this decision must have been painful. Though still vigorous, Parquin was now fifty years old and could recall three Bourbon regimes, two revolutions, an Orleanist monarch and, above all, Napoleon. To his delight Louis Napoleon proposed a morning ride together in the woods. On their arrival at a clearing, a favorite spot in previous years, the two solemnly dismounted. The prince explained that it was "here that the voice of a brave soldier of the Grand Army awakened in my spirit the first dreams of glory." Since here he "began to be conscious of the grandeur of my name and of the responsibilities it imposed.....I wanted it to be here that I tell you what I am planning....This heritage of the great Emperor, which belongs to me, shall be claimed by force."

Emotionally moved, Parquin took Louis Napoleon's hand and kissed it. Then slowly and precisely Louis explained his plans, concluding, "Are you with us?" Parquin answered, "Prince, through life and death."

They then agreed that Parquin would request an extended leave and take some trips to Strasbourg where he had maintained contacts from his service as gendarmerie commandant six years earlier. All preparations would be ready by mid and late October. Parquin's final departure for Strasbourg was on October 24, one day ahead of Louis Napoleon. On the same day, six days before the coup, his Wolfsberg estate was sold to an Englishman.

Between June and October 1836, while Louis Napoleon and Persigny were lining up supporters, Franco-Swiss relations steadily worsened over the issue of Switzerland as a haven for revolutionary plotters. In late June the Swiss made a gesture of capitulating by agreeing to expel some political refugees, sending them to the French border. The French ambassador, the Duke of Montebello, huffily suggested that Germany, Austria and Italy should receive their own revolutionaries. The Conseil episode erupted in July, leading to Swiss threats against Montebello and on August 29, the demand for his recall, just eleven days after Voirol had warned his government of an "imminent" military movement by Louis Napoleon.

In Paris on September 6, 1836, the Thiers ministry gave way to one headed by Molé. French threats over conspiracies hatched in Switzerland by political refugees continued until, on September 27, 1836, diplomatic relations were broken. Charging the Swiss for succumbing to "criminal influences", the French threatened invasion, establishing a camp of eight thousand men near the border and advancing two brigades toward Ferney on the outskirts of Geneva. This deterioration of Franco-Swiss relations may have been a factor in Louis Napoleon's timing of the coup.

Despite political refugees being in the diplomatic spotlight, prominent relatives and visitors continued to come and go from Arenenberg, including Colonel Amable de Girardin of the cuirassiers at the New Breisach garrison, de Bruc, and Napoleon's youngest brother, Jerome and his son.

Sensing a real danger of being caught up in a broad net cast to appease the French, in early October Louis Napoleon met in Berne with leaders of the Swiss Executive Council. After noting that as a respected honorary citizen and a captain in the Swiss army he had every right to reside in the country, he declared that he would leave Switzerland rather than be the perceived cause of danger for the country. Hortense was, of course, in a particularly exposed position and it was imperative that she appear to have no knowledge whatever of her son's coming adventure. In view of heightened French pressure for the Swiss to expel trouble-makers, if Hortense were perceived as an accomplice in the coup, then surely she would again be in her untenable position of 1815, an uprooted and wandering exile. It remains to this day a question whether or not Hortense knew of the developing plot. Almost unanimously historians have maintained, as did Louis Napoleon, that she did not. However, even Laure de Franqueville had known of the plot for four months and many others also knew. Persigny had been part of the Arenenberg household for over a year, and with the increased activity in the summer of 1836, Hortense would have to have been terribly naïve or incredibly preoccupied not to be informed. In this context is an intriguing suggestive undated letter from Louis Napoleon found among Parquin's possessions. Written at Arenenberg and hand-delivered to Wolfsberg, the prince wrote, "How happy I will be to acknowledge someday your devotion to the national cause. I am going to discuss all of this with mother…" It is difficult to believe that she was completely unaware of what was going on.

On October 10 Louis dined with Jerome, de Bruc and a number of others at Aarhu west of Zurich. Jerome then left for London and de Bruc for Paris by way of Strasbourg. A week later de Bruc was with Persigny in Strasbourg. By chance he met Falloux, a casual acquaintance, as Falloux was leaving a theatre. Falloux later said he happened to be in Strasbourg on his way back to Paris after a visit to the deposed Bourbon Charles X, who was then close to death in Gorizia. De Bruc led Falloux to Persigny and the two friends embraced enthusiastically. Once again Falloux declined an invitation to join the plot though he professed to be intrigued by the idea.

In mid October several generals on whom Louis Napoleon still thought he could rely were informed that the prince had an important communication for them and a rendezvous was suggested in the Black Forest later in the month. Following up on this contact, by the 20th de Bruc was in Paris, using the name of Bayard and staying in a hotel rather than his own home. He was the bearer of two letters: one from Persigny to Madame Gordon, presumably then in Paris; the other from Louis Napoleon to General Count Remy Joseph Isadore Excelmans. At the Return from Elba Excelmans had been the officer who took charge of the Tuileries for Napoleon on March 20, 1815 after Louis XVIII had fled. The approach to this particular general was markedly unsuccessful.

Excelmans declared that the prince was misleading himself if he believed he had a following in France; there was great veneration for the emperor, but that was all. De Bruc's offer to take him to Arenenberg in his own carriage was declined outright.

On the 25th of October, Louis Napoleon left Arenenberg for Strasbourg. He allegedly told Hortense he was going to meet some political friends and then spend a few days hunting. However, as he was about to leave, Hortense put on his finger Josephine's wedding ring from Napoleon as a good luck charm in case he were to encounter danger, surely a recognition on her part that this was no ordinary departure.

In the late evening of the 28th Louis Napoleon entered Strasbourg with a passport identifying him as Auguste Oppenmann, a proprietor from Rixheim. Accompanied by his servant Charles Thélin, Louis had spent much of the previous three days, as the Baron de Dietfurt, in the area near Freiburg, meeting with fellow conspirators at the hotel L'Homme Sauvage. Eleonore Gordon and Colonel Vaudrey were there, registered as M. et Mme. de Cessey. They had arrived from spending a month at Vaudrey's country home near Dijon, from which Gordon had made a quick trip to Paris. De Bruc, registered as Bayard, was there from Paris and Persigny, as Manuel, joined them from Strasbourg. The hoped for Black Forest meeting never occurred as no generals showed up, a last minute disappointment. Louis was also in Lahrs, New Breisach, Colmar and possibly Besançon, before finally arriving at Strasbourg with a trunk full of his portraits and biographies. He stayed at accommodations already rented for him in the Rue de la Fontaine, close to the Austerlitz barracks as well as Querelles' quarters at 4 Rue des Orphelins, which were serving as a general headquarters for the conspirators.

By the 29th all the major participants had gathered in Strasbourg save de Bruc who was in Freiburg. Louis Napoleon walked openly in the streets of Strasbourg and in the early evening Persigny brought Vaudrey to meet him on the Quai Neuf. The colonel was later to claim that this was when he decisively agreed to participate in the coup; but this story of a last minute decision can hardly be given much credence, considering the previous few months. The two hour meeting was not crucial for Vaudrey's decision but important nonetheless. At this eleventh hour Vaudrey persuaded Louis Napoleon to make an apparently minor change in the plan which had already been carefully devised.

Many meetings and countless hours had been devoted to the question of where the prince should make his first appearance. From the locations of the quarters of the various units it was clear the first efforts should be concentrated on the two artillery regiments, pontonniers and the 46th infantry. But which should be approached first? From a strictly military view, the 3rd artillery made the most sense. It was centrally located with its field pieces ready at hand, while the ordnance for the 4th was a considerable distance from its barracks. Louis Napoleon, however, did not want a coup based on the intimidation of real military power. He clung to his idea that it should be based on the inherent popularity of his name and that that would ultimately lead him to power without bloodshed – as had been the case for his uncle in 1815. Accordingly, the collaborators finally agreed that he should appear first to the 4th artillery. Its Napoleonic connection was unique and Vaudrey was also in more direct control. After winning it over he should lead it from the barracks (Austerlitz) to the 46th infantry in the Finkmatt barracks, on the opposite side of town. Meanwhile, engineering officers and officers of the 3rd artillery in the town's center would rally their units, while printed proclamations were being plastered on walls throughout the city. From Finkmatt barracks the growing force would go via the Jewish area and Place St. Nicolas to the 16th infantry at the Citadel where Louis Napoleon would read his proclamation to all the assembled units. After thus gaining overwhelming garrison support, any authorities not joining them would be arrested.

Vaudrey's suggested modification was that after leaving

Austerlitz barracks with the prince at the head of the 4th artillery, Louis Napoleon and Vaudrey would go together to the headquarters of the garrison commander, General Voirol. He would be arrested at that time if he did not collaborate and the group would then continue to Finkmatt barracks. This, however, required Parquin and Persigny to be involved in the arrest of Voirol as well as Choppin-d'Arnouville and also would slow the march to Finkmatt.

Louis Napoleon approved the revision believing, he later confided to his mother, that it would offer the garrison commander "not a dagger at his throat, but the eagle before his eyes." Vaudrey assured the prince of success as the two collaborators audaciously strolled on Strasbourg's Pont Neuf. Their brazen public appearance alerted neither civil nor military officials as they polished their seditious plans not far from both the prefect and the garrison commander.

After meeting with Vaudrey Louis Napoleon joined about fifteen of the other accomplices at 4 Rue des Orphelins. Assembled there from the Strasbourg garrison were Major Jules-Barthélemy Lombard, Lieutenants Louis Dupenhoat, Gros, Pétri, Couard, and Poggi. Others present included Parquin, Laity, Persigny, Gricourt, Querelles, recently discharged Lieutenant A.N. de Schaller, and two Alsatian garrison officers recruited by Parquin, Colonel Brice of Haguenau and Colonel de Girardin of New Breisach.

During the cold October night Louis Napoleon wrote two letters to his mother, one to be sent in case of victory, the other should the enterprise fail. He also dictated proclamations to the French people, to the army, and to the citizens of Strasbourg. These were signed "Napoléon," the name he often took after the 1831 death of his older brother, a procedure decreed by Napoleon after the death of Hortense's first son in 1807. Most of the collaborators spent the night in nervous conversation. Meanwhile, a light snow settled over the city.

Chapter Six

The Abortive Coup

On Sunday morning at five o'clock, October 30, 1836, Colonel Vaudrey left his quarters near the Place St. Etienne and proceeded to Austerlitz barracks. Within an hour he had the regiment mustered in the courtyard, in dress fatigues and weapons in hand. The troops were totally surprised at this call to arms on a Sunday morning and further amazed at the distribution of ten rounds of ammunition to each soldier as well as eight or nine sou (about ten cents) apiece. Vaudrey also ordered horses to be watered and fed since he did not know when or if, the regiment would be returning. Orders also were sent to the 9th battery at Saverne, about twenty-five miles northwest of Strasbourg, to take arms and be alert until further notice. At six o'clock he entered the courtyard, viewed the regiment, drew his sword and, while motioning towards the gate, observed to his staff, "Now, gentlemen, the moment has arrived. We shall see if France still remembers twenty years of glory."

In an adjacent street Louis Napoleon waited with a number of his followers. He wore a blue artillery uniform with red collar and braid, epaulettes of a colonel, the Legion of Honor medal, a straight sword of the heavy cavalry and a general staff army hat. As he thoughtfully looked over his associates, Parquin, Persigny, Gricourt, Lombard, Querelles, and others, a voice called out, "Forward, Prince. France follows you." As he entered the courtyard, welcomed by a drum-roll from the regimental band, Vaudrey addressed the regiment:

> Soldiers of the 4th artillery, a great revolution
> begins at this moment under the auspices of the

> nephew of Emperor Napoleon. He is in front of
> you and he comes to lead you. He returns to his
> native land to regain rights for the people, to recov-
> er glory, which his name evokes, for the army, and
> to restore freedom to France. He depends on your
> courage, your devotion and your patriotism to
> accomplish this great and glorious mission.
> Soldiers, your colonel has answered for you; repeat
> with him, Vive Napoléon! Vive l'Empéreur!

The response was dramatically enthusiastic. The prince indicated that he wanted to speak and Vaudrey re-established silence. With
a firm voice Louis Napoleon reminded the assembled men of the
emperor's special association with their regiment. He had served the
4th artillery as a captain and with the 4th he had fought at Toulon.
The 4th had opened the gates of Grenoble to him when he returned
from Elba; and now, new destinies were in store. They would
receive renewed glory for this beginning of a great venture, as they
followed the eagle of Austerlitz and Wagram! Taking the standard
from Querelles, Louis held it high.

> Soldiers, here is the symbol of French glory, des-
> tined in the future to become also the emblem of
> freedom. For fifteen years it led our fathers to vic-
> tory. It has waved over every battlefield. It has been
> in every capital of Europe. Soldiers, Rally to this
> exalted flag. I entrust it to your honor and to your
> courage. Let us march together against the traitors
> and oppressors of our country, shouting, Vive la
> France! Vive la Liberté!

He had barely finished when an electrifying emotion galvanized
the entire regiment. With raised swords they repeatedly and unanimously cheered, "Vive l'Empéreur! Vive Napoléon!" These shouts
such as Parquin never heard even from the old Imperial Guard filled
him with awe and excitement. The magic of Napoleon's name,

unleashed by the mere sight of his nephew and the imperial eagle, overwhelmed and encouraged the prince. His judgment about Bonaparte sympathies on the part of the rank and file was clearly accurate. He had won over more men than his uncle had on the Return from Elba.

The regiment divided into four detachments with Louis Napoleon's officers deftly taking command and separating to carry out their assigned duties. Major Lombard took a squad to produce proclamations at the printing plant of a Gustave Silbermann, an active opponent of the July monarchy. At the Rue Sainte-Catherine, a few blocks from Austerlitz barracks, Persigny was detached with a platoon to arrest the prefect; another platoon with Lieutenant Pétri was sent to secure the telegraph office. Officers from the 3rd artillery rushed to assemble their men. Louis Napoleon ordered Lieutenant Schaller to take a dozen artillerymen and arrest Colonel Leboul commander of the 3rd artillery, and also General Lalande, commandant of the Department of the Lower Rhine. At this point another officer was sent to rouse the 46th infantry at the Finkmatt barracks. Eleonore Gordon watched all this activity from the gate, then returned briefly to her room at the Hotel de la Ville de Paris. Meanwhile, a courier was sent to Arenenberg conveying the message that the coup was successful. Hortense was awakened at 2 a.m. Monday morning, the 31st, with news that her son was the master of Strasbourg. She at once shared this news with servants and guests, none of whom noted that she was surprised or shocked.

At Strasbourg Louis Napoleon had assumed full command and, with Vaudrey, Parquin, Querelles, Gricourt and other officers, led the 4th artillery out of the compound and headed for the Finkmatt barracks by way of the administrative heart of the city. Despite the early hour, citizens crowded around them and joined the soldiers' shouts: "Vive Napoléon! Vive l'Empéreur!" Vive la liberté!" At times Louis Napoleon was so surrounded by supporters that Colonel Vaudrey's mounted artillerymen had to clear a path for him. Men rushed forward to embrace the eagle held by Querelles.

With great excitement townspeople, brewers, bakers, butchers, and soldiers accompanied them past the gendarmerie, where the guard turned out, presented arms, and shouted, "Vive l'Empéreur!"

Even General Voirol's servants enthusiastically shouted with the crowds – and opened wide the commandant's gates. As a precaution artillerymen surrounded the quarters, although Vaudrey appears to have believed the prince had already secured Voirol's cooperation. Despite the general's rebuff when approached earlier by letter, Louis Napoleon was confident that this demonstration would revive the old soldier's Bonaparte sympaties and that he would join the movement.

Awakened by the noise, the general was not yet fully dressed when Louis Napoleon, Vaudrey and Parquin entered his room. Astonished, Voirol began to berate Vaudrey whom he held personally accountable. Seeing that the colonel was unmoved, Voirol turned to Louis Napoleon, exclaiming, "Prince, they have deceived you!" Personally indebted to Louis Philippe, the general remained firm in his allegiance to the Orleanist monarch. Despite this emphatic rebuff, Louis Napoleon judged from Voirol's subsequent words and actions that the episode caused him to be painfully torn. The unsuccessful confrontation disturbed Louis Napoleon. Voirol's emphatic loyalty to Louis Philippe had surprised him, but respecting the general's service to his uncle, rather than imprisoning him with the prefect, he instructed Parquin and a dozen artillerymen to keep him under house arrest.

Meanwhile, excitement among the troops and populace continued to mount. Crowds met Louis Napoleon and Colonel Vaudrey as they emerged from the commandant's quarters, their acclamations blending with those of the 4th artillery. With the regiment's infantry guards in the lead and the band playing the *Marseillaise*, Louis Napoleon, Vaudrey and their enthusiastic following resumed march to the nearby Rue du Faubourg de Pierre to rally the 46th infantry at the Finkmatt barracks.

Only two approaches led from the broad Rue du Faubourg de

Pierre to the barracks. The men could go either straight north to the ramparts leading to Finkmatt, or they could turn to the east on a narrow passage, the Rue Graumann, lined with numerous houses and buildings leading directly to the courtyard's main entrance.

An approach by the narrow street had been rejected during the planning since only four men could march abreast, thus forcing Louis Napoleon to appear at Finkmatt with only a small unimpressive escort, while most of the regiment was left ineffectively standing in the Rue du Faubourg de Pierre and not demonstrating to the 46th that an entire regiment had already been won over. An approach by the ramparts, however, would enable him to appear with all of the enthusiastic 4th artillery. He could address the entire infantry regiment assembled in the long narrow courtyard between the barracks and the ramparts and the ramparts would also provide an advantageous withdrawal route. If the 46th did not accept him, fifty mounted soldiers could bar the single barracks gate on the north while men on the ramparts pulled back. The force could then move to the Place d'Armes, there joining the 3rd artillery and still have force enough to ensure success.

As the column marched up the Rue du Faubourg de Pierre, Louis Napoleon remained preoccupied by the general's negative reaction while his most reliable aides—Persigny, Laity, and Parquin – were performing assigned tasks elsewhere. As originally planned, Persigny had been designated to lead the column up the Rue du Faubourg de Pierre to the ramparts because he was intimately familiar with the streets of Strasbourg. However, in another late change Louis had diverted Persigny to arrest the prefect, judging Choppin-d'Arnouville's "energetic character" a potentially serious obstacle. Parquin also was familiar with Strasbourg's streets, but he was still with Voirol and neither Querelles nor Gricourt were familiar with this section of the city. As a result the column was headed by men from the 4th artillery and, being accustomed to the most direct route, they turned into the narrow Rue Graumann instead of proceeding to the ramparts. Accordingly, Louis Napoleon entered the barracks area with a following of barely four hundred men. The bulk of these were left outside the gate to secure a retreat if need be, and the prince entered the courtyard with most of his "staff" and only a small escort. This unfortunate development was compounded by another fateful circumstance. Louis Napoleon had expected to see the regiment already assembled, but for some unknown reason, the officer earlier assigned to inform them of the events at Austerlitz had not yet arrived and no preparations had been made. Unlike the 4th artillery, no officer in the 46th had been committed beforehand, and many were like that unit's Captain Morin who, when asked, "Why are you not with us, you who wear a cross from the Emperor?" replied, "I was at Waterloo but this young man is not the Emperor!" Less prone than ordinary troops to respond to an emotional appeal to treason, such officers had no difficulty in loyally serving the existing regime.

The hour was still early on this Sunday morning and the men were in their quarters preparing for inspection. Attracted by the noise in the courtyard, they peered out the windows. The prince, modifying his prepared address, called up to them, briefly identified himself, and sketchily stated his mission. Hearing the name Napoleon, they dashed out pell-mell and surrounded him. An old sergeant-major of the imperial guard broke down in tears, rushed towards him, seized his hand, and kissed it. Young and old followed. Soon cries of "Vive Napoléon! Vive l'Empéreur!" filled the Finkmatt courtyard.

On the brink of success, Louis Napoleon and his officers organized several infantry companies. Men from both the infantry and artillery congenially mingled. Shortly, the engineering battalion and the 3rd artillery regiment were expected and then Louis would have three regiments and five thousand men for his march on Paris.

Despite Voirol's opposition and the mistake on the proper route, the plot seemed to be unfolding successfully. Unfortunately, more problems and miscalculations were in store. At various locations throughout Strasbourg, Bonapartist officers were busy attracting support or trying to suppress dissent. Lieutenant Laity had mustered six companies of engineers. Though they were shouting "Vive l'Empéreur!" while marching towards the Place Saint-Etienne, en route to Finkmatt about half of them decided to drop out. Overcoming opposition from an adjutant major, Lieutenants Dupenhoat and Gros managed to get the 4th and 12th engineering companies assembled. Lieutenant Schaller easily arrested both General Lalande and Colonel Leboul. However, General Lalande escaped through an unguarded door and headed for the Citadel to alert the 16th infantry. Lieutenants Poggi and Couard secured the 3rd artillery's arsenal and, joined by a number of sympathetic officers, led the regiment from its barracks. Lieutenant Pétri had met no obstacles in seizing control of the telegraph office and Major Lombard was busily producing hundreds of proclamations.

Meanwhile, Persigny arrested Choppin-d'Arnouville and took him, dressed only in a light robe and trembling from fear and cold, to the Austerlitz barracks. Arriving there only forty-five minutes after he had left with the regiment, Persigny turned the prefect over to a warrant officer of the 4th artillery, Victor Jacquet. Telling him to put his prisoner in the dungeon by orders of Colonel Vaudrey, Persigny twice warned the young officer that he would answer with his head if the prefect escaped. Despite these specific orders, when Choppin-d'Arnouville complained about strong odors, Jacquet moved him to an officers' room. Guarded by a sergeant and a sentry, one in the room and the other in the corridor, the prefect was only to spend an uncomfortable half-hour being detained.

Colonel Parquin, however, had trouble. In a general's uniform, he generated allegiance from the artillerymen, who accepted his authority over Voirol. When the general had appeared at his door and told the soldiers they had been deceived, Parquin simply responded "Vive l'Empéreur," and Voirol had retired to his room. Impressed with Voirol's objections, however, Parquin locked the door.

Incredibly, with thirteen men guarding him, the general still managed to escape to the street through an unlocked and unguarded door. Parquin pursued him and a scuffle ensued. Voirol's shouts of "This general is a traitor, a scoundrel. Kill him!" fell on deaf ears. Voirol subsequently reported to the minister of war that the "faithful and brave cannoniers….listened to me" enabling him to get a horse, whereupon "saber in hand" he went to the Citadel where he "was assured of finding a faithful regiment, the 16th of the line." In fact he had not met "faithful and brave cannoniers" who helped him, but Parquin and then Eleonore Gordon who met him with a pistol in each hand. Unfortunately, she believed him to be a supporter of the coup and thus he was not prevented from making his way to the Citadel. She later declared she would have killed him had she known the truth. Meanwhile, Parquin headed for Finkmatt to tell Louis Napoleon the bad news.

How could Gordon have thought Voirol supported the coup? At the confrontation had he indicated he supported the prince? She had sung in his home and knew him; she must have had some reason to believe in his support. Could it be that in previous private conversation he had not been as emphatically anti-Bonapartist as his contacts with Louis Napoleon's emissaries suggested?

By this time the prince had begun to have trouble. At the opposite end of the Finkmatt courtyard, a commotion started and rippled through the soldiers. Initially, Louis Napoleon could not identify the origin. The regiment's commander, Lieutenant Colonel Marie Claude Félix Talandier, a loyal Orleanist, had been warned just in time by none other than Franqueville who, awakened by noise in the street, had rushed to Voirol's and when the chips were down, followed his commander's lead. Talandier's quick thinking was to be the decisive factor in the coup's failure. He skillfully rallied his infantry, shouting "You have been tricked. The man who is stirring you up is nothing but an adventurer, an imposter." This fiction was reinforced by other staff officers with Colonel Paillot adding, "He is not the nephew of the Emperor; he is the nephew of Colonel Vaudrey. I know him."

This buzzed from man to man. In only a few minutes the regiment's reception perceptively changed. Believing themselves deceived, they became outraged; Louis Napoleon and his men vainly tried to assuage them while Talandier ordered the gates closed behind them.

The unexpected accusation jolted Louis Napoleon. Since his birth as a Prince of the Empire, nobody had ever questioned his identity, although he had tried to conceal it on occasion. To him it was simply unthinkable for a stranger to question who he was. His name, his position as the Bonaparte heir – the cornerstones of the coup – disappeared with a few words and dissolved his support. Momentarily shocked, Louis Napoleon could not immediately comprehend such an abrupt change in those friendly to him moments earlier.

Elements of the two regiments, confined in the narrow barracks courtyard, antagonistically jostled. Confusion, disorder, hostility and rivalry between the two military branches intensified. Artillerymen arrested infantry officers; infantrymen seized artillerymen. Weapons were loaded, bayonets were fixed, swords were drawn.

Talandier worked his way towards Vaudrey, who remained by Louis Napoleon, and the two colonels drew swords. Vaudrey shouted, "Artillerymen, defend me!" Louis Napoleon ordered the infantry officers arrested; the 46th defended them. The infantry took Vaudrey prisoner; the artillery rescued him. One man from the 4th regiment was wounded in the defense of his colonel. A veritable massacre could have materialized; but still believing his name and heritage alone would carry the day, Louis Napoleon refused to sanction armed force as well as an offer from Querelles and Gricourt to force a passage for him. Instead, he hurled himself into the midst of the infantry in a desperate attempt to win them back. Encircled by bayonets, he drew his sword to parry their thrusts. Artillerymen, seeing the danger he was in, rescued him and prevented French soldiers from killing the emperor's nephew. As Louis Napoleon later wrote to his mother, "Then all was confusion."

Now separated from his officers, he became enveloped by those who did not acknowledge him as Napoleon's heir. Striving to procure a horse and be above the confusion, he lunged towards the few cavalry present. Infantrymen repulsed him, shoved the horses back against the wall, and took him prisoner. Unable to defend him, his officers submitted.

Meanwhile, portions of the 4th artillery left in the Rues Graumann and du Faubourg de Pierre became restless as the rising pandemonium convinced them their colonel and Louis Napoleon had encountered opposition. Shouting angrily against the infantry, they crowded against the gates, their noise joining the confusion in the courtyard. Meanwhile on the ramparts a large number of civilians gathered, shouting "Vive l'Empéreur" as they threw stones at the 46th.

At this point Colonel Parquin arrived, sized up the situation, and resolving to die rather than abandon Louis, entered the melée, trying to reach the prince. The old veteran defended himself until he was seized and led to Colonel Talandier, who ripped off his epaulettes and sneered derisively, "You are a traitor and a wretch!"

Colonel Vaudrey meanwhile was surrounded by artillerymen. Talandier threatened "Surrender—or you are dead!" Backed by the 4th, Vaudrey defied him. The tense confrontation ameliorated when Talandier appeared to back down. Taking an oblique approach, he shouted above the din, "Silence . . . I want to speak to the Colonel."

Distracting Vaudrey, Talandier convinced him the people believed he supported the Duke of Bordeaux and a Bourbon restoration. Caught off-balance like Louis Napoleon earlier, Vaudrey reeled upon hearing this bizarre supposition. Confused and hopeless and with the prince already captured, he gullibly accepted Colonel Talandier's preposterous assertion, succumbed, and gave his last major command, "Artillerymen, retire. Return to quarters. Obey the laws." He dispatched an officer to tell Eleonore Gordon that all was lost and then followed Talandier into an officer's room in the barracks.

On the ramparts Persigny and Laity surveyed the scene. The 3rd artillery was beginning to disperse and Louis Napoleon, Vaudrey, Parquin, Querelles and Gricourt were all prisoners. Citizens continued to shout, "Vive Napoléon!" and to stone the infantry while the 46th fired random shots to disperse them. With the 4th driven back against the ramparts, infantry and artillery still faced each other in fury. Horses nervously pranced between them. The 46th pointed bayonets at the chests of the artillerymen. Weapons loaded, the 4th prepared to fire.

"Vive l'Empéreur! Vive le neveu de Napoléon," the artillerymen shouted. "That is not him," responded the infantry. In an attempt to defuse the crisis some officers opened wide the gates so the artillerymen might more readily leave the area. As they began to filter out, Laity and Persigny ran to them, urging that they get their field pieces. The prisoners could be released, the defeat turned around. This rekindled elements of the 4th who futilely started towards the artillery park before realizing that only Colonel Vaudrey, now a prisoner, could release shells from the arsenal. The coup had sputtered to an inglorious end – barely three hours had elapsed since its beginning.

• • •

With the vision of hindsight, it is evident that, despite a number of encouraging factors, there were many others which contributed to the coup's failure.

Louis Napoleon's judgment was probably correct that Strasbourg's garrison and population were well suited as a site for a coup. Louis Philippe's position was clearly insecure and the prince's ideas were sound on the general impact of the Napoleonic Legend in the nation at large, especially among the army's rank and file. Beyond this, however, he may have expected too much of the Legend. Its potential for providing support from officers was far more questionable. As a group they were more aware of their career perspectives than regular troops and also more sensitive to the implications of duty and treason. Louis Napoleon brought to his judgments far too much in the way of idealistic emotion. While the memory of the emperor and his Legend were omnipresent in his own life, it was not the case to most other people. Above all, the greatest handicap perhaps was the obvious fact that Louis Napoleon simply was not Napoleon Bonaparte, especially in character, instincts or in other peoples' estimation.

The over-all planning for the coup, despite all the time devoted to it, had been neither careful nor secretive enough. By approaching too many people indiscriminately, too many knew of the scheme. It was further a mistake to rule out the use of force completely. Here Louis Napoleon's sentimental faith in the power of the Legend was simply unrealistic. He also was not a good enough judge of people and too prone to hasty assessments, as in the case of Raindre. He was obviously too optimistic about Voirol and his failure to realize what Franqueville would do when the moment of crisis came is telling. For the task at hand Louis Napoleon probably had too few dedicated conspirators and too few officers were at the higher ranks.

A glaring failure was the lack of more preparatory work in the 46th infantry regiment. Further, a higher priority and more care should have been given to having the 46th mobilized in time. Also deserving more attention was the important role the 3rd artillery could play. In addition to Louis Napoleon and Vaudrey, the plans should have assured that Parquin and Persigny remained with the main force on its progress to Finkmatt. For the wrong approach to have been taken even after the issue had been discussed was an incredible blunder. For Generals Voirol and Lalande to have both escaped through unguarded doors also reflected failures in planning.

A final factor in the coup's failure related to Talandier's presence of mind and ridiculous fabrications. Neither Louis Napoleon nor

Vaudrey proved intellectually flexible enough to react effectively to the unpredictable. Only Eleonore Gordon was to show any such ability.

Reminiscing about the coup's failure, an optimistic Louis Napoleon was to write, "I am firm in my belief that if I had followed the plan which I had marked out for myself, I should be in my own country." He saw no basic defects in the plan and never dwelt on specific technical failures in carrying it out.

Nonetheless, despite all the shortcomings in the plan and its execution, the coup had enjoyed initial success and it was certainly appropriate for Louis Philippe and his ministers to have been alarmed.

Chapter Seven

Immediate Aftermath

Word of the capitulation spread quickly and at the Silbermann printing plant Major Lombard began destroying the proclamations he had just produced. He then left Strasbourg and made his way by carriage to Arenenberg. There, on Monday the 31st, Hortense learned for the first time the bad news. Also on the 31st de Bruc finally arrived in Strasbourg.

Meanwhile, Persigny and Eleonore Gordon were at 17 Rue de la Fontaine burning piles of the prince's portraits, biographies and other compromising documents. Four gendarmes arrived to arrest Persigny, but Eleonore's quick thinking and opposition enabled him to escape. She pretended to faint and asked for some smelling salts. Persigny leaned towards her long enough for her to tell him about an unguarded door. When the gendarmes started to seize her trunk, she cried, "Give me this trunk. It contains my money and my papers" and struggled to retain it. Convinced the papers were important, the gendarmes were diverted from Persigny who fled. That evening he met briefly with Charles Thélin and then, in disguise and with a servant, made his way to an inn in a small village near Offenburg. He was harried from there by gendarmes who seized his servant, their horses and personal belongings. Wandering alone on foot in the Black Forest, he hid for a while in a friend's house. Finally, he reached Arenenberg and a month later with a false passport left for England where he wrote his account of the Strasbourg affair. Unlike Persigny, Eleonore Gordon – either from loyalty to Vaudrey, to Louis Napoleon, or perhaps to both – stayed in Strasbourg and was arrested.

After Louis Napoleon was apprehended, he was hustled into the barracks guard-house. Parquin was already there, his hands bleeding from the melée in the courtyard. Startled, the prince exclaimed, "You are wounded. You have shed your blood for me!" Parquin replied, "I wish there was not a drop of it left in my veins. I wish you were safe at home with the Queen at Arenenberg…Prince, we shall be shot, but it will be in a good cause." Querelles was likewise steadfast, declaring, "Prince, notwithstanding our defeat, I am still proud of what we have done." When Louis Napoleon asked Vaudrey if he could ever forgive him, the colonel simply responded "Yes" whereupon the prince remarked "at least, I will not die in exile." Ironically, that was exactly his fate.

With the insurrection disintegrating both Voirol and Choppin-d'Arnouville were free and a wave of arrests began. At this point Voirol wrote the ill-fated telegram which created so much anxiety for the king and his ministry in Paris. Keeping all the prisoners under his jurisdiction until either Paris or Procureur General (Attorney General) Rossée from the Alsatian judicial center at Colmar could take over, he transferred Louis Napoleon to the Citadel and saw to it that he had a room with a window and was given whatever he wanted except his freedom.

Throughout the city rumors galore were circulating, including one that both Franqueville and his wife Laure were accomplices. Actually at 8:00 a.m. during the height of the insurrection Laure had written her sister Fanny that "my poor Aimé will be the first exposed" and three hours later "I do not dare to write Valerie for fear of compromising my husband." Voirol, however, dismissed any accusation against his aide and, proving his trust in Franqueville's loyalty, dispatched him to Paris with a brief letter to the minister of war summarizing what had occurred.

Franqueville rode almost continuously in rain mixed with snow for nearly 48 hours to cover the 488 kilometers from Strasbourg to

Paris, arriving at 10:00 a.m. on Tuesday, November 1. He was rushed immediately to the Tuileries and there Voirol's letter was read aloud, revealing what the telegram had concealed. Louis Napoleon and his accomplices were imprisoned in Strasbourg, not marching on Paris. Although General Voirol admitted that at the moment he was too busy and excited to write a full report, he tried to reassure the government by sending this message by his aide-de-camp "post-haste" to Paris to report that his soldiers remained faithful to Louis Philippe. Nevertheless, his hasty description of "this deplorable circumstance" and of the "insurrection" of the 4th artillery disturbed the ministers who proceeded to interrogate the exhausted Franqueville for some five to six hours.

Barely an hour after Franqueville's arrival, a special mid-day edition of the *Moniteur* appeared. In addition to a succinct statement concerning the "criminal attempt" of Prince Louis Napoleon Bonaparte, it reported the emergency ministers' meeting, reprinted the October 30 telegram, included a list of eight participants (Vaudry, Parquin, Gricourt, Laity, Querelles, Louis Napoleon, Eleonore Gordon and a sergeant Boisson) and Voirol's letter to the war minister. The urgency and uncharacteristic speed of the government in distributing news of the failure lent substance to the later opinion of Odilon Barrot that the initial rallying of Strasbourg to Louis Napoleon was "serious" and "not the desperate act of a foolhardy pretender."

From Paris, Lebel, director of the Conciergerie (prison) was sent to Strasbourg to take charge of the prisoners for the government. Arriving on the scene, he at once judged that Louis' situation at the Citadel was too lax and he ordered his transfer to the city prison. There, however, the best room was prepared for him and this was where he remained until the decision about his immediate future was made in Paris.

At the capitol, the ministers debated various punishments. Although Guizot had opposed the emperor and was one of the few ministers not formally affiliated with the Empire, he now joined the others in advocating leniency for Louis Napoleon. "The heir to the name and . . . to the throne of the Emperor Napoleon out to be dealt with as of royal race, and subject only to the exigencies of politics." Molé had spent many days of his early manhood in the salons of Queen Hortense and argued that Louis Napoleon should be ranked in a special category, such as that accorded the Duchess of Berry who had been pardoned after her coup attempt in 1832.

Who would condemn the nephew of the emperor? Most of the ministers had served Napoleon. Would they serve as executioners of a Bonaparte? Several peers, uneasily anticipating having to serve as judges, protested to the king. Eighty generals and superior officers also objected to a trial. The final unanimous recommendation of the cabinet was that Louis Philippe should pardon Louis Napoleon, advice which the king accepted. Forty years earlier, as an exile himself, he had voluntarily gone to America. Why not send a Bonaparte there now? It would appear humane and it would avoid the risk of an acquittal by any court. If he could have felt assured of a conviction, he could pardon after a verdict. But he felt no such assurance.

At Arenenberg Hortense responded to the early news of the coup's success with a letter to her son urging moderation and mercy. She conveyed no hint of surprise or consternation and the message carries a strong implication that she was aware of the plan. When imprisoned Louis Napoleon tried to further the myth (alibi) that Hortense was ignorant of his scheming, writing on November 1 as much for the authorities as for Hortense, "My dear mother, . . . you who believed I was at my cousin's." When Lombard arrived on the 31st with news of the failure, Hortense was calm while several servants despaired and talked of all kinds of dire consequences, including a need to flee before an Austrian invasion! As Hortense and her companions discussed the situation, one imperative emerged: somehow, the life of the prince must be saved! Since the coup was entirely military, a council of war would surely judge him and he could be shot in twenty-four hours!! Madame Salvage de Faverolles thought the only way to save Louis Napoleon was through bribery:

"Thirty, forty, one hundred thousand francs, give it, promise everything, but save him!" Hortense decided to send Valerie Masuyer to Strasbourg bearing two hastily written letters, one to Louis Philippe and one to General Voirol. Possibly the general could be persuaded to help. "A former general of the Empire would not want the Emperor's nephew's blood shed! . . . Perhaps he would render a service to the King by letting him escape." That evening Valerie crossed Lake Constance with a servant and headed north to Strasbourg bearing the letters as well as some shirts for Charles Thélin. Two days later Hortense decided that no avenue should remain unexplored and that she must try to intercede directly. Accordingly, with Madame Salvage she left Arenenberg for the chateau of the Duchess of Ragusa at Viry near Paris. After writing Louis Philippe and Molé asking for clemency for her son, she met with Molé who told her of the decision to deport him to America.

Late in the evening of November 1, after twenty-four hours of cold fatiguing travel, Valerie arrived at a hotel in Strasbourg where she was given "a bad supper, a small room, and a hard bed." On the 4th she moved to an auberge at Kehl, just across the Rhine. Interestingly, she made no effort to stay with her father or her sister Laure. Contacting General Voirol she learned that both he and his wife were upset about the potential fate of Louis Napoleon. Madame Voirol was especially solicitous. She arranged for her maid to deliver the shirts to Charles Thélin and conveyed letters from Valerie to Louis Napoleon and also Laure. She also gave Valerie the key to a gate leading to her private garden and advised her to use that entrance in the evening for the day's news. This same day Valerie had the first glimmer of hope for Louis Napoleon. She wrote Hortense that Laure had received a letter from Franqueville in Paris, reporting that he believed the prince would not be shot and also that nobody seemed to think that Hortense was involved. Laure was still upset about her husband being suspect and believed that both she and Valerie were also suspect and might well be on the verge of being arrested. She viewed the situation as dangerous and unsettling. Valerie's mere presence was disturbing and it was risky for Laure to see or write either of her sisters. Escape plans for the prince were pondered but none appeared practical. Meanwhile, appalled by the "catastrophes" and upset that his daughters were implicated, Dr. Masuyer left for Paris, hoping that he might somehow help.

On the 4th Valerie observed that "all of the city is struck with terror. Everything becomes more tense. Soldiers engage in duels. The trial will be held in Strasbourg." Two days later she received a gratifying letter from one R. Coze, a friend of an attorney for the king. He reported that the ones being blamed for the coup were Louis Napoleon's accomplices. They had misrepresented the state of affairs in France and had urged this young Bonaparte to do something rash. Therefore, Louis Napoleon would simply be detained, but his friends would be put on trial.

The next day, November 7, Valerie left the Strasbourg–Kehl area and headed for Arenenberg. She had done all she could but was desolate that Hortense had left for Paris with Madame Salvage on the 2nd. She felt the trip was unnecessary and that the queen seemed not to trust her. From Haslach she wrote Madame Salvage, offering to join Hortense in Paris. Snow and bad weather hampered her trip but she arrived at Arenenberg on November 9. When only servants were on hand to meet her, she was sure she had lost the confidence of Hortense, not realizing that her letter announcing her return had been intercepted by the police.

Interesting recriminations began to surface. Ex-King Jerome indignantly canceled all marriage plans between his daughter Mathilde and Louis Napoleon. Valerie Masuyer now saw Madame Salvage as insinuating herself into a position replacing herself as Hortense's closest companion. She also reconsidered her doubts about Parquin – perhaps it had been General Voirol who had led the prince astray. Laure continued to lash out at Parquin and even Vaudrey. Persigny questioned Parquin's loyalty, a query which actually denoted jealousy and reflected more on Persigny than Parquin.

Laure made lavish excuses for her husband who certainly was among the culpable. She described the whole episode as a masquerade – the prince disguised as the emperor and Parquin disguised as a general. While even Louis Napoleon was not sure Valerie had not compromised the plan, her own family perceived her, along with Madame Salvage, as among the scheme's collaborators. Valerie's position was indeed tenuous and Laure plaintively inquired, "What are you going to do? Will you be able to live in Switzerland?"

In Strasbourg at 8:00 in the evening of the ninth, Lebel turned Louis Napoleon over to Voirol and Choppin-d'Arnouville who were presented with orders from the ministers of war and the interior respectively. No explanation was given to the prince who requested that he be allowed to stay with his companions. They politely insisted he go with them. Perplexed, he only learned he was being taken to Paris when the carriage with two guards pulled up beside him. In the presence of these escorts, Commandant Guinot and Lieutenant Thiboulot, he complained about being separated from his accomplices and later wrote that he feared only one thing: clemency from Louis Philippe. The two guards transferring him from Strasbourg to the Paris Conciergerie were former officers of the Empire and close friends of Parquin whom they held in high esteem. They treated Louis Napoleon with such kindness, he wrote his mother that "I could have thought myself traveling with friends."

Arriving in Paris at 2:00 in the morning on Saturday, November 12, he was met by Gabriel Delessert, the prefect of police and an old friend of Hortense. Delessert told him that she was with Madame Salvage at the chateau of the Duchess of Ragusa at Viry, and added, "The King is giving you a full and complete pardon." Louis Napoleon again protested not sharing the fate of his friends, declaring "I want to be judged."

From prison he wrote to Louis Philippe and to his mother. To both he protested about receiving clemency while his friends were still imprisoned. "I am, Sire, alone guilty; it is I who has brought about their recalling memories of past glory." Mildly chastising

Hortense for interceding, he wrote, " . . . you did not think of my honor, which obliged me to share the fate of companions in misfortune. I feel a great grief in being separated from men whom I led to their destruction, when my presence and testimony might have influenced the jury in their favour."

Louis Napoleon had only two hours in Paris before leaving for Lorient, a journey of nearly three days. With neither rest nor a change of clothes, he was escorted to the port city by the same guards who had brought him from Strasbourg to Paris. Taken first to the citadel of Lorient, after four days, on November 19, he was transferred to the citadel across the bay at Port Louis. All communication to him was forbidden but he was permitted to write letters. While waiting at Port Louis for a "favorable wind," he wrote an old friend, Narcisse Vieillard, a captain of artillery during the Empire and tutor to his older brother, "I am leaving, heart-broken at not being able to share the fate of my companions in misfortune. I wished to be treated as they were treated . . . I shall know how to bear this new exile with resignation; but I am in despair at the thought of leaving in prison men whose devotion to the Napoleonic cause has been so fatal to them." As a gesture of royal kindness Louis Napoleon was given 15,000 gold francs immediately prior to his departure, though it should be noted that on his capture the government had confiscated 200,000 francs from him. On November 21 at one-o'clock in the afternoon, Louis Napoleon boarded the frigate *Andromede*, the ship that would be his home for four months.

Louis Napoleon was not the only one upset with Louis Phlippe's decision. His release produced much reaction. Royalists lamented that it raised a Bonaparte to the dignity of a Bourbon. Odilon Barrot, who offered to defend the young Bonaparte, criticized the pardon as "indiscreet." The secrecy of the release was assailed. Only on November 12, as Louis Napoleon was on his way to Lorient, did the news break that he had been in the capital and that Queen Hortense had tried to intercede for her son. The press spot-lighted the issue of equality before the law and probed the reasons for the special treatment. The *Nouvelle Minerve*, protesting Louis Napoleon's "exceptional category," editorialized that fear was the motivating factor. At a trial the skilled Barrot could stir great and dangerous memories, provoking embarrassing questions. The *Journal des Debats*, taking the opportunity to object to the exile of Bonapartes ("deprived of rights accorded to the humblest citizens") also believed fear of an acquittal motivated the king's pardon. Whatever Louis Napoleon had done, the glory, the name, the memory of the emperor, the public conscience, and a sense of delicacy would all prohibit a trial. Above all, a jury "would be bewildered and frightened" if selected to judge Napoleon's nephew.

By removing the major defendant, the king had revealed his apprehension. Uncertain of controlling the Napoleonic Legend and Bonaparte popularity, Louis Philippe had prudently decided this nephew of the conqueror should be kept incommunicado from court, press and accomplices. At the same time the government spread word, and kept repeating, that Louis Napoleon had pledged to never again return to France as part of the bargain for his release. Despite the fact that this was false and was emphatically and repeatedly denied by the prince who had been pardoned "without conditions," it became part of the standard Orleanist account of the coup.

At Colmar Procureur General Rossée had not been informed of the pardon or the release. Louis Napoleon had left Strasbourg for Paris on Wednesday evening, November 9; members of the court at Colmar did not learn of his departure until the following day when they found out by chance rather than through official channels. Expressing his astonishment, Rossée was told, "The government has initiated great and important policy by sending Louis Napoleon to the United States, but it intends rigorous justice in the prosecutor's application of laws to the accomplices." Nevertheless, the procureur-general formally protested this "exceptional act of high government policy."

While Louis Napoleon's fate was already decided, that of his friends was still being debated. Which court should handle the accomplices? The Court of Peers? A military court? A jury of the people in a civilian court? Could it be logical to allow a "simple jury" to decide the punishment for superior officers involved with a plot concerning the name of Napoleon? If soldiers alone had been involved, the case would have been tried by a council of war. Although the coup was essentially a military crime, it also involved civilians and former military personnel. This ruled out a trial before a military tribunal. In a conspiracy involving civilians either the Court of Peers or a jury must judge.

Guizot believed Louis Napoleon's accomplices should be tried by the Peers. "That court alone was capable of appreciating the propriety" of pardoning the nephew of the emperor. Unencumbered by any sense of idealistic equality, the Peers would punish the Strasbourg accomplices in an "appropriate" manner.

Pressured by public insistence on a jury trial, Louis Philippe acquiesced. "Crimes of this nature,," his council of ministers boldly announced, "deserve prompt justice." However, Rossée was convinced that an Alsatian jury would acquit the prisoners and recommended a major change of venue. The minister of justice, Persil, was caught between these views but felt unable to cede before such "vain terrors" and refused the change of venue. Apprehensive nonetheless that an acquittal could mean his own resignation, he insisted that the whole affair should absolutely be over by January 1. He further advised his subordinates to avoid the time-consuming danger of trying to prove everything and of futilely attempting to find all the accomplices.

Hoping to minimize the scope of the October attempt, early charges against Charles Thélin, de Bruc's wife, Lieutenants Couard, Poggi, Cavel, Lafond, and de Geslin were dropped. Only thirteen were then charged with committing a capital offense, including Lieutenants Dupenhoat, Pétri, Gros, Schaller, Major Lombard and Persigny. However, several thousand had participated; about fifteen garrison officers had avidly supported Louis Napoleon and actively engaged in the planning. Of these only Vaudrey and Laity were arrested and charged. Reluctant to disclose the conspiracy's extent, the government did not indict twenty-five who invaded the prefect's bedroom, and then arrested, humiliated and imprisoned him in the Austerlitz barracks. Only one person, Parquin, was arrested for seizing the garrison commandant although he had been accompanied by at least twelve artillerymen from Vaudrey's regiment. In the end only seven were imprisoned for "this horrible crime"; for six the government demanded death, de Bruc being the exception.

When the trial began on January 6, 1837, the coup's leader who – according to government charges – precipitated the potential "civil war," "European war," and "disastrous consequences" was confined on a French frigate approaching Rio de Janeiro. Louis Philippe had sent sealed orders, to be opened only after several weeks at sea, to the ship's captain that the trip to America be made by way of Brazil. He thus prohibited Louis Napoleon's public visibility by a circuitous route which kept him at sea for over four months. Prudent measures, but hardly those of a confident monarch.

In the meantime the Strasbourg garrison experienced a number of transfers and promotions. Among these Voirol was removed from command and put on a leave of absence but raised to "the dignity of a peer of France" (a baron); Talandier became a full colonel; Francqueville was promoted to lieutenant colonel; the prefect, Choppin-d'Arnouville, though regarded by the ministry as the one mostly to blame for not realizing the gravity of the plot, was nonetheless elevated within the Legion of Honor; and a number of NCOs were summarily discharged.

Chapter Eight

The Coup And The Courts

On January 6, 1837, five days after Persil had wanted the affair terminated, the trial of Louis Napoleon's accomplices began at Strasbourg's Palace of Justice, only a few blocks from the Finkmatt barracks. Public interest and support for the defendants ran high; and each day before daybreak fervent Alsatians appeared, some with lanterns, and jostled for position to be admitted to the courtroom.

The prosecution was headed by Procureur General Rossée, aided by three associates. Although Rossée was Alsatian and had been identified by the minister of the interior in 1833 as an associate of republicans, on this occasion he proved to be zealous in pressing the government's case. His colleagues were far more moderate.

Before leaving France Louis Napoleon had written to his mother, Louis Philippe, Odilon Barrot, Vieillard, and to Vaudrey. To all he protested being separated from his fellow accomplices and especially objected to the clemency and pardon. He asked Hortense to see that all was done to help the prisoners in Strasbourg and also to see to the care of Vaudrey's two sons, then in Paris with their mother. Louis Napoleon's letter to Vaudrey suggested some arguments which might be used in his defense, but it was addressed in care of Rossée who may not have forwarded it to the colonel. The letter to Odilon Barrot was a long catalogue of points which he felt the lawyer could use in defense of his associates as well as explaining his own actions. He wanted the jury to know that he regarded it as his right to be able to defend himself in court; also they should know that after 1830 he had asked to return to France as a citizen and to serve in the army as a simple soldier; and that at Strasbourg his goal was to convoke a national congress and to have a constitution as in America and England. He shouldered all responsibility for what had occurred – "I alone prepared everything" – to such an extent that he substantially overstated his role, ignoring, for example, the substantial part played by Persigny, to say nothing of Vaudrey. Odilon Barrot had volunteered to defend Louis Napoleon but when it came to defending the others, he delegated this chore to his brother, Ferdinand, also a noted lawyer.

The attorneys for the defendants were thus led by Ferdinand Barrot, spokesman for Vaudrey as well as the absent Louis Napoleon. An ardent legitimist and learned former law professor at the University of Strasbourg, Thiériet, came out of retirement explicitly to represent Laity. Parquin's attorney was his brother, Jean Parquin, an ardent Orleanist and, according to Louis Blanc, a "celebrated member of the Paris bar." Defending de Bruc and Eleonore Gordon was Louis Liechtemberger who had a reputation in Alsace of "virtue adorned by talent." Querelles was defended by a republican, Martin, then at the beginning of an illustrious career, and Chauvin-Beillard, a legitimist, defended Gricourt. It was an impressive legal group and constituted a substantial advantage for the defense.

Throughout the trial the prosecution faced not only distinguished legal opposition but also major fundamental problems in the nature of its case. Omnipresent in the minds of all was the failure of the government to even indict Louis Napoleon, and his preferential treatment went far to jettison its position. It was abundantly clear that he was the leader of the coup and the one most responsible. That he was not among the accused and had been pardoned was seen as a royal policy grounded more in fear than generosity or justice and lent an aura of hypocrisy to the government's case. The leader of the simultaneous, failed Vendôme revolt, Brigadier (corporal) Bruyant, had just been tried by a council of war at Tours and sentenced to death, a judgment Louis Philippe changed to deportation. A final difficulty for the prosecution was its insistence that, rather than being the ringleader and instigator of the coup, Louis Napoleon was a stranger to France and seduced by his accomplices who needed a famous name to shield their evil purposes. Vaudrey yearned to be a lieutenant general or a marshal while the others also sought either promotions or money. This rationale proved simply unconvincing.

The jury selection process resulted in a body containing both republicans and legitimists. In this border city it naturally numbered some who did not speak French and so the entire trial took place in both French and German, a tedious process which extended the whole proceedings. Prominently displayed through the trial for all to see, including the jury, were two tables of evidence, including a virtual homage to the emperor in the form of his Grand Cordon and Star of the Legion of Honor worn at Austerlitz and also his gold-handled sword from that epic triumph.

The seven defendants entered the courtroom from an underground passage. Taking seats in a row were Vaudrey, Parquin, Laity, Querelles, Gricourt, Gordon and de Bruc. Five of the group were officers or former officers and several wore their uniforms and decorations. The exception, of course, was Eleonore Gordon. Only Vaudrey and Laity were from the Strasbourg garrison and only Vaudrey and Parquin over thirty years old. All sat erect giving no indication whatever of contrition.

The procureur general began his case with an extended attack on the missing Louis Napoleon. Rather than discrediting the prince, his remarks, replete with sarcasms and innuendo, piqued the curiosity of the jury members who heretofore actually knew relatively little about this particular Bonaparte's background. Condemning his tenacity, Rossée claimed the pretender "nursed a chimerical dream" to restore his uncle's empire. Even before the death of the emperor's son, the 1830 French revolution gave Louis Napoleon "fresh hope" and an "eager attitude." Delighted defense attorneys seized on the absurdity of the prosecution's allegation that Louis Napoleon had deviously settled close to France in a Swiss chateau to foment trouble. Noting that he had been only a youngster when he was moved to Switzerland, the defense also reminded jury members of limited Bonaparte options after banishment from France.

The prosecution denounced Louis Napoleon for being one of the first to provide "form and direction" to Italian revolutions. Persevering even when "broken with disease" and devastated by the death of his only brother, personal adversities were "not enough to master him." Rather than damaging Louis Napoleon, this oratory led the jury to perceive Louis Napoleon as an admirable martyr. Rossée's sarcasms were incomprehensible to the somber, attentive jurors. Denigrating "the warrior" posing as a "legislator," he condemned Louis Napoleon's proposed constitution for advocating democratic rights and for seeking adherents "on all sides and in all classes of society." "The young soldier whose sword had just been broken in Italy seized his pen," wrote political and military works, scattering them throughout France. Cavalierly dismissing the 500 page *Swiss Artillery Manual* as "another brochure," Rossée mentioned that in *Political Reflections* Louis had claimed that only Bonaparte blood could regenerate France. The jury reflected on his "considerable perseverance" in contacts with French officers and wondered at the government's assertion that he "easily found discontented men" - - a peculiar admission.

Incredibly recollecting the Return from Elba in this era of Napoleonic romanticism, the prosecution reproached Louis Napoleon for "stirring the imagination" of Frenchmen "by dwelling on the glories of the Empire", a practice of Louis Philippe himself. The prince and his companions had carried Imperial Guard swords, clearly revealing intentions to use force in implementing a democratic constitution. Such incriminating "evidence," presented as sinister by the government, appeared laudatory to engrossed jurors and courtroom spectators, who transformed the prosecution's hostile recitation into a catalogue of admirable attributes.

The defense called the jury's attention to why Louis Napoleon was absent, Ferdinand Barrot rhetorically asking, "Why is he absent? Has he fled? ... No gentlemen, a thousand times NO. He desired your justice; he demanded it." Accusing the government of sending Louis Napoleon to America simply for political expediency, he read from a letter Louis Napoleon had written on November 11 protesting being separated from his companions and fearing that his absence at a trial might weaken their defense. "Gentlemen of the jury, if you saw on the bench of the accused a prince of the blood of Napoleon, a nephew of the conqueror of Austerlitz, for the honor of France you would not condemn him and, in his acquittal, he would carry us along with him." To such oratory the prosecution acknowledged that the prince had "emitted complaints" about "unjust" treatment but lamely maintained that his absence was a "political necessity" and that "the sovereign has the right to pardon."

Colonel Vaudrey was presented by the prosecution as vain, immoral, and ambitious. To the jurors, however, this fifty-two year old officer appeared dignified and distinguished. Enrapt jurors listened to Barrot's review of Vaudrey's impressive military career. Then Vaudrey delivered his personal testimony. To an attentive court and audience he claimed that Madame Gordon was the only other defendant that he knew, having first met her on June 20, 1836 when she gave a private concert at the home of General Voirol. He conveniently never mentioned his subsequent relationship with the singer.

Learning of Louis Napoleon's plans at Baden in July of 1836, the colonel testified that he tried to dissuade the prince at this first meeting. This portion of his testimony may have been close to the truth. He had indeed raised questions then about the scheme and most accounts agree that Vaudrey's whole-hearted support was withheld until mid-October. Barrot reminded the jury that this coincided with increased French pressure on Switzerland – including a military threat – which had increased Louis Napoleon's anxiety about the uncertainty of his being allowed to live so close to the

French frontier. Moved thus by a sense of near desperation and with the colonel as an adherent, Louis Napoleon had gone ahead with his plan for a coup. This explanation had a core of truth adorned with elements of half-truths. Vaudrey insisted that he had resisted until late in the evening of October 29th, when he became "carried away" after two hours with the prince. He mistakenly believed General Voirol acquiesced or, at least, would not oppose them. When the court president queried about any ulterior plans, Vaudrey simply replied, "The Prince wished to make an appeal to the people." This straightforward response caused a sympathetic stir in the courtroom.

The next defendant to testify was Lieutenant Laity who, according to Louis Blanc, spoke with a candor which excited stronger interest than any other prisoner. Acknowledging his part in the preparations for the "democratic revolution" of October 30, 1836, Laity bluntly declared, "I am a democrat and a republican." When earlier told Louis Napoleon could rely on France and the army, he affirmed, "I believed it and believe it still!" When questioned about the sincerity of his oath to the French government in light of his pledge of loyalty to Louis Napoleon until parted by death, he calmly responded, "I had sworn fidelity to my country, but not to the Prince who misgoverns it." Both he and Vaudrey vigorously denied prosecution charges of promised promotions as motives. Laity insisted that he followed Louis Napoleon "only because I found in him democratic opinions." With prompting by Thiériet, he then proceeded to tell in graphic detail his part in the uprising. At its end he had an opportunity to escape but preferred to accept his comrades' fate. With "noble despair" he ran "to share the disaster of the Prince, whose fortunes he could not save." His testimony was moving and sobs were heard in the courtroom. Outside, cries of "Vivent les opinions du Lieutenant Laity" echoed in Strasbourg streets.

The third of the seven defendants to testify was the forty-nine year old Colonel Parquin. With his blue coat and large Legion of Honor rosette, the handsome Parquin made a marked impression on the jury and the audience, his devotion to the emperor's memory having "singular force." Respecting Louis Napoleon's defense letter claiming all responsibility, he falsely stated that he first heard of the plot when he saw the prince at noon on October 29.

Parquin dismissed his oath to the Orleanists as simply routine compared to his oath to the emperor in 1804, four years before Louis Napoleon Bonaparte was born. He insisted he respected oaths, unlike "a certain great diplomatist who has sworn thirteen" - - a reference, perhaps, to Talleyrand. The 1804 oath, however, "remained graven" in his heart for over thirty-three years; Parquin regarded himself bound by it "the day when the eagle reappeared, the day when the nephew of the Emperor came to me and summoned me to keep my oath." He defended his oath as being "sanctioned" by four million votes; "I don't think that foreigners and traitors have the right to bind me by another." Parquin's loyalty to Napoleon and to the imperial eagle produced such applause and emotion that the court president threatened to restore order by clearing the courtroom.

Parquin's earnest demeanor, vigorous descriptions of October 30 events, and his glove blood-stained from a bayonet thrust, made significant impressions on the public and jury alike. Unlike Vaudry who vehemently contradicted Talandier's fabricated assertion that he had seized him by the collar, Parquin did not object to Talandier's account of tearing off his brigadier-general's epaulettes (which he had worn less than three hours).

Jean Parquin produced one of the most touching portions of the trial. Similar to Barrot's defense of Colonel Vaudrey, he was impassioned when discussing his brother's contributions to the glory of the Empire. Reminding the jury again of Louis Napoleon's youth when Hortense bought Arenenberg, he went on to relate his own experiences at the home of the former Queen of Holland. Witnessing his brother's marriage to Mlle. Cochelet in the small chapel on the chateau grounds, he claimed to have been impressed even then with the young nephew of Napoleon. The lawyer praised his "kindly nature, his rare and brilliant qualities, his affection for the country in which he was born and his resemblance to the valiant captain whose nephew and adopted son he was," skillfully playing on the Napoleonic sympathies of jury members. His oration ended with an emotional plea that his mother could stop her worrying because an Alsatian jury would surely acquit her other son (the colonel).

Viscount Lieutenant de Querelles followed Colonel Parquin and echoed his account of what had transpired on the 30th, but from the perspective of one who had carried an eagle which had belonged to the 4th infantry, reminiscent of Grenoble in 1815. When asked how the emperor's nephew was able to inspire him when he was too young to have known Napoleon, he responded that he was moved by a "strong sympathy for a brave and noble young man." Like his predecessors, Querelles maintained the justness of the planned coup and admitted that implementing it was the only reason he happened to be in Strasbourg on October 30. His defense counsel indignantly objected when the prosecution charged that Querelles unseemly motive for following Louis Napoleon was simply money. Querelles himself specifically denied participating because he expected it to lead to a promotion. When asked upon what basis he placed his hopes for the success of such a plot, he responded, "on the general discontent which was evident in the whole army," causing a stir in the courtroom. He declined to mention specific officers but maintained that the conspirators had the promised support of senior commanders.

The testimonies of Querelles, Gricourt, and de Bruc tended to be interlaced as the prosecution tried to determine their prior contacts with each other, with Louis Napoleon and Persigny, and also their movements prior to October 30. Thus there were a number of instances where defendants interrupted the questioning of others with clarifications or denials.

In the courtroom Count Gricourt made a striking appearance, dressed in a blue dress coat with gold buttons and a black and blue floral patterned vest over an artistically folded shirt ruffle. Since Gricourt and the escaped Persigny were designated as captains of Louis Napoleon's so-called General Staff, the prosecution spotlighted them as particularly important.

When Captain Raindre testified about his meeting with Louis Napoleon and his skepticism about the prospects for a coup, Gricourt interrupted to state that contrary to Raindre's remarks, his enthusiasm for the idea had given special encouragement to Louis Napoleon. Raindre's rejoinder that if the prince were present, he would verify every word of his testimony, provided an opportunity that Jean Parquin could not resist to interject that "It is the great misfortune in this affair that the Prince is not here." At this point the court curtly dismissed Raindre's testimony as irrelevant, even though the prosecution had regarded him as an important adjunct to testimonies by Franqueville and Voirol.

One of the more frightening attempts on the life of Louis Philippe was the Fieschi affair on July 28, 1835. Inferring that Gricourt and de Bruc had some connection with the episode even though both at the time were with Louis Napoleon at Arenenberg, the prosecution produced Captain Edouard de Geslin, identified also as a property owner in Paris. De Geslin said the plot had twice misfired before and that Gricourt and de Bruc were involved with Persigny over a year before October 30 in an effort to bribe him to assist in overthrowing the government. He would become a general and there would be no lack of money. Gricourt contradicted much of the story and called de Geslin nothing but a usurer. When the president of the court observed that a generalcy was a pretty substantial ("fort bel") advancement, de Geslin claimed that to him it would have been simple justice since he had served as an officer since 1802 but that anyway he had refused the offer.

When the prosecution asked Gricourt about Louis Napoleon's plans for the French throne, he replied, "Prince Louis never thought of placing himself on the throne. Love of country is the most powerful feeling that animates him." Subsequently Gricourt interrupted the examination of a military witness to declare that the prince told him, "Not a drop of French blood shall be shed." On the seventh day of the trial, the prosecutor scornfully singled out Gricourt, de Bruc and Gordon as leading Louis Napoleon "into error" for their own monetary gains, an allegation the defense duly protested.

The interrogation of Eleonore Gordon differed substantially from that of the other defendants. She was poised and somewhat austere with piercing eyes, black hair and wearing a white satin hat and dress of black silk with a heavily embroidered lace collar. Though she was involved in and knew much of the coup's planning and details, she revealed very little and admitted only to helping Persigny destroy papers in the wake of the coup's failure. The government in fact had very little against her and its attack on her consisted mainly of a host of scornful innuendos: she was an immoral public singer, a money hungry, intriguing adventuress, a mistress of Persigny and later Vaudrey, accusations and smears indignantly denied by defense attorneys.

The last defendant, Frederic Count de Bruc, wore a blue dresscoat buttoned to the neck adorned with the ribbon of the Legion of Honor. His auburn hair had been carefully combed and his demeanor was solemn. The prosecution had not demanded the death sentence for him since he was not in Strasbourg during the coup. The other defendants had been defiantly proud of what they had done, but de Bruc appeared far less dedicated and tried to distance himself from the others.

De Bruc claimed only to have met Louis Napoleon momentarily at Aarhu where the prince asked him to deliver a letter to General Excelmans. He failed to mention other occasions when he met Louis Napoleon and others involved in the plot. The bulk of his testimony related to the letter to Excelmans which intrigued the prosecution. Excelmans was the most prominent of approximately ninety witnesses called to testify and he was specifically asked about the letter. He confirmed receiving the letter and claimed that he told de Bruc to inform Louis Napoleon that there was no Bonapartist party in France and "to dissuade him from any such project." This reference to a "project" implied that the general, like many others, was aware of the plans being contemplated for Strasbourg. Also, like others, he had failed to alert authorities in Paris and after the trial, the government introduced a bill proposing imprisonment for any who, knowing of a plot against Louis Philippe, failed to inform authorities.

In Louis Napoleon's letter to Excelmans asking for a meeting, one sentence especially intrigued the court. He referred to the letter's bearer, de Bruc, "who deserves my entire confidence." This gave an impression that de Bruc was more involved than he pretended and neither Excelmans nor de Bruc gave a satisfactory explanation of why the prince had such "entire confidence" in him.

The trial centered naturally on the seven defendants but the parade of other witnesses provided more details of the events of September 30 though little more about the planning. Rossée and his colleagues respectfully implied that the motive of money explained the defendants' actions, while the defense similarly referred to the government's actions which prevented the prince from being present. The testimony contained a number of interesting exchanges. Captain Raindre was sanctimonious and enthusiastic in portraying his great sense of loyalty to Louis Philippe and of the way he "confounded" the prince and tried to talk him out of the planned coup. "I thought all I had heard so foolish that . . . there was no danger in keeping it a secret … so I held it to be my duty to put myself in communication with the authorities."

During Voirol's testimony, Vaudrey requested that the court ask him if Louis Napoleon had not seemed surprised when the general refused to accede to the developing coup. Voirol replied that rather than surprise the young prince appeared terrified, a reaction supported by no other witness. The question of why Vaudrey and others had believed Voirol would not oppose a Bonapartist coup was never probed nor explained during the trial. Also not explored was why Voirol did not convey to Prefect Choppin-d'Arnouville the information which Raindre had provided. Also unexamined was Franqueville's position in the whole affair, his testimony being limited to Voirol's reaction to Louis Napoleon's first approach to him by letter. An entertaining aspect of the trial was the boatful testimony of Talandier who gleefully told how he had hoodwinked Vaudrey by telling the colonel the people thought the revolt was for Charles X and that they would tear him to pieces.

At the end Rossée solemnly reminded the jury that the issue was not one of a "common crime" but of an "organized revolt … against the realm, a call to the throne of a man who is not himself French, in spite of his name." On January 18 the case went to the jury. The last moments had been tense, with the spectators calling for a judgment of acquittal. The jury withdrew and took only twenty-two minutes to acquit all the defendants on all counts.

Announcement of the verdict sparked instant celebrations, in the courtroom and in the city. Strasbourg had a holiday appearance and a duel between Talandier and Parquin prolonged the carnival air. Highlighting the mood of excitement was a banquet held for the acquitted defendants; and at the artillery school at Metz, a notorious center of republicans, there was a special reception for Laity and Gordon.

Meanwhile French public feeling against Louis Philippe reached "a fearful height" and in the Chamber of Deputies his government was the subject of a "vigorous harangue." As a consequence of the "scandalous" acquittal, it had proposed a bill punishing crimes committed jointly by military men and civilians, the former to be tried by councils of war, the latter, ordinary tribunals. The opposition to such a procedure was immediate and widespread. A bill to send persons guilty of the same crime before different judges appeared to be an attempt at a "cruel revenge" for Strasbourg, a "work of anger," and the government was rebuked with a quotation from the emperor himself: "Justice is one in France; a man is a citizen before he is a soldier."

There appeared to be little middle ground between reactions to the verdict. *Le Courrier du Bas-Rhin* applauded the jury for giving victory to the great principle of equality of all before the law. *Le National* and *La Charte de 1830* found the verdict both just and equitable. To Metternich on the other hand, the acquittal was "a deplorable event." Lamartine denounced the verdict as an "unparalleled scandal" and declared himself "amazed and indignant over so much favor shown to such daring rebels."

A shakeup of the government saw Gasparin replaced as the primary scapegoat and Guizot and Duchatel both resigning in protest. At the same time Montebello in Berne was chastised for not having informed Paris of the coming coup at Strasbourg, though such a warning from Voirol had not resulted in its prevention.

• • •

On April 15, 1837, the same day Molé's government was reconstituted, Louis Napoleon finally arrived at New York, after landing on March 30 at Norfolk. In New York he was met by his servant Charles Thélin and also Count Arese, a friend and accomplice during his Italian exploits and subsequently a frequent visitor at Arenenberg. He tried to make contact with his uncle Joseph, but was rebuffed. He seems to have had no contact either with Lucien or Achille Murat, also in America, or with Elizabeth Patterson, first wife of Jerome, or her son (Louis Napoleon's cousin) Jerome Bonaparte. Nonetheless, the exiled prince readily adapted to New York and made a host of friends among the city's elite, including Washington Irving and James Fenimore Cooper.

Louis Napoleon's American sojourn came to an abrupt end in early June when he learned that his mother was now seriously ill, diagnosed with advanced cancer. After a hasty letter to President Van Buren apologizing for not having time to pay his respects in person, he left New York on June 12. In London July 10 he was delayed by passport problems before he finally arrived at Arenenberg on August 4. Thus Hortense and her son had two emotional months together before she passed away on October 8, 1837.

To escape the memories haunting Arenenberg, Louis Napoleon

moved a short distance to an old lake shore castle, Gottlieben, which he had inherited from his mother. During the winter of 1838 he restored the castle which had earlier incarcerated Jean Huss as well as Pope John XXII. To the indignation of the French, his guests at Gottlieben included Persigny, Laity and other participants in the Strasbourg coup.

Accordingly, the French renewed pressure on the Swiss government to expel Louis Napoleon. The Swiss however testily ignored the demands to turn against this Bonaparte who had lived in their midst since childhood. The federal government merely referred the matter to cantonal authorities. French threats only made the Swiss more defiant and Louis Napoleon more popular. A banquet in his honor was given by forty-five Swiss officers at Kreuzlingen on May 20, 1838. Three days later the Thurgau Marksmen elected him president of their annual muster at Diessenhofen. Praising them for their bravery and independence, Louis Napoleon declined the honor, gently explaining that his words would be misinterpreted and his intentions misconstrued, rendering his service ineffective.

In 1838 Louis Napoleon and Laity decided to respond publicly to the pressure and the propaganda the French government had been distributing during the eighteen months following the trial. Contradicting all the distortions from Paris, Laity, with Louis Napoleon's help, wrote *Relation historique des événements du 30 October 1836: Le Prince Napoléon a Strasbourg*. This was a descriptive work which contained no hint of apology but justified and even glorified the coup. Only one author's name, M. Armand Laity, identified as a former lieutenant of artillery and student at Polytechnic School, was on the title page, but Louis Napoleon acknowledged his collaboration. He revised the narrative himself, incorporated personal letters and endorsed Laity's published account "as the exact truth." His participation also accounts for why Laity's book is markedly better than Persigny's.

In addition to both earlier letters and later statements, there are several other indications of Louis Napoleon's authorship. A quotation from Thiers' classic on the French Revolution, used by Louis in a postscript to one of his letters a year earlier, was on Laity's title page, "Every party that is compelled to act in the dark, is reduced to expedients which are called intrigues - when they are not successful." The book also revealed the French government's earlier intention to banish to America not only Louis Napoleon, but also his mother Hortense since she was then in Paris, allowing her no time to arrange her affairs. Whether true or not, the inclusion of it is indicative of Louis Napoleon's hand, rather than that of Laity. Another issue, primarily of importance to Louis Napoleon, was also included. Hortense was allegedly requested to pledge assurance that her son would not return to Europe for ten years. Refusing to make such a pledge, she responded that he alone was master of his actions. Time after time, Louis Napoleon was confronted with accusations that he broke his word of honor. Outraged by attempts to discredit him, he persistently disavowed - - even ten years later at Ham in 1846 - - the government charge that he or his mother broke such an oath.

Published in Paris in June 1838, the 95 page book quickly sold 10,000 copies, reminding everyone of the coup and restoring Louis Napoleon Bonaparte to prominence. It also resulted in the arrest of Laity.

On June 21, 1838, Laity was apprehended and charged with a crime against the security of the state, an action itself which indicated the seriousness with which the government regarded Louis Napoleon's Strasbourg coup. Laity's book was considered politically dangerous and its distribution was forbidden. *Le National* protested Laity's arrest, on the basis of freedom of the press. Article seven of the enlightened Charter of 1830 was explicit, "censorship can never be established," and the law of October 8, 1830, mandated trials by jury for all press offenses. However, after Fieschi's attempted assassination of Louis Philippe in 1835, the repressive September Laws were enacted, allowing press offenses to be tried by a Court of Peers. Laity's trial was the first application of the new laws. Louis

Blanc objected to Laity being denied a jury trial and branded the arrest as clearly an arbitrary punishment "for correcting certain historical errors in narratives of the Strasbourg affair, and for having done homage to glories of the Empire and for having spoken of Louis Napoleon with affection." The *Courrier français* pointed out that the ministry had made a young man often publicly regarded as foolish into virtually a national hero.

In Paris the city's police were placed on alert lest Louis Napoleon attempt another coup. Moving with uncharacteristic speed, the government was able to get Laity's trial started on June 28, only a week after his arrest. Four days after the trial began, Louis Napoleon wrote to his imprisoned friend:

> You are, then, to go before the Chamber of Peers because you have had the generous devotion to reproduce the details of my enterprise, to justify my intentions, and to rebut the accusations of which I am the object. I cannot understand the importance which the Government attached to the suppression of this pamphlet. You know that in authorizing you to publish it my only object was to repel the cowardly calumnies with which the Ministerial organs covered me during the five months I was in prison or at sea. My honour, and that of my friends, were concerned in proving that it was not a mad dream which led me to Strasbourg in 1836. They say your pamphlet is a fresh conspiracy, while, on the contrary, it acquits me of the reproach of ever having conspired; and you state in the early pages that we waited two years to publish the facts concerning me, so that the public mind might be calmer, and that men might judge without hatred or prejudice.
>
> If, as I like to believe, a spirit of justice animates the Court of Peers, if it be independent of the executive power, as the Constitution directs, it is not

possible that you can be condemned; for, I cannot too often repeat, your pamphlet is not a call to revolt, but the simple and true explanation of a fact that has been misrepresented. I have no other support in the world than public opinion, no reliance except in the esteem of my fellow-citizens. If it is impossible for you, and also for me, to defend myself against unjust slanders, I shall regard my fate as the cruelest possible. You know my friendship for you well enough to understand how grieved I am at the idea of your falling a victim to your devotion; but I know also that, with your noble character, you will suffer resignedly for the popular cause.

You will be asked, as certain journals are already asking, Where is the Napoleonic party? Answer, 'The party is nowhere – the cause is everywhere.' The party is nowhere, because my friends are not brigaded; but the cause has partisans everywhere, from the workshop of the mechanic to the council chamber of the King, from the soldiers' barracks to the palace of the marshal of France – Republicans, Juste-Milieu, Legitimists, all who desire a strong government, real liberty, an imposing governing authority. All these, I say, are Napoleonists, whether they know it or not; for the Imperial system is not the bastard imitation of English or American Constitutions, but the governmental form of the principles of the Revolution. It is a hierarchy in a democracy, equality before the law, reward for merit; it is, in short, a colossal pyramid with a broad base and a high head.

Say that in authorizing you to publish the pamphlet my aim was not to disturb the tranquility of France, nor to rekindle smouldering passions, but to show myself to my fellow-citizens as I am, and not as the hate of interest has depicted me. But if some day parties were to overthrow the actual Government (the example of the last fifty years make this supposition permissible) and, if, accustomed as they have been for the last twenty-three years to despise authority, they were to sap all the foundations of the social edifice, then, perhaps, the name of Napoleon would be a sheet anchor for all that is generous and truly patriotic in France. It is for this reason that I insist, as you know, that the honour of the eagle of October 30 shall remain intact in spite of its defeat, and that the nephew of the Emperor shall not be taken for a common adventurer. You will be asked, no doubt, where you obtained all the statements you publish; you may say that you received them from me, and that I certify on my honour that their truth has been guaranteed to me by men worthy of belief.

Adieu, my dear Laity. I should put hope in justice if the interests of the moment were not the only morality of parties.

Receive the assurance of my sincere friendship.

Louis Napoleon

On July 9, 1838, eleven days into the trial, a public session was held. The indictment by the prosecutor, Frank-Carré, vigorously condemned Laity's insolence: a mere eighteen months after standing trial for an armed attempt against the French government, Laity not only had justified the attempted revolt, he glorified it; he wanted to legitimatize the conspiracy and the whole Strasbourg attempt of 1836; he exalted his cause, directly provoked and invoked a future conspiracy to establish Louis Napoleon Bonaparte on the throne; to soldiers, he conjured up memories of glory; to the people, he recalled the power of France; to timid men, he presented an easy revolution. The prosecutor portrayed Laity's book as a party manifesto, a program for another attempt.

According to Frank-Carré, the government had wanted to believe the Strasbourg affair nothing more than the desperate act of some officers, and Louis Philippe had wanted to make it appear in history as simply a humiliating blunder by Louis Napoleon Bonaparte. Unfortunately, Laity's publicity of Napoleonic ideas had demonstrated that Louis Napoleon was unwilling to accept this version of events. On July 10, 1838, less than three weeks after his arrest, Laity's trial ended. Unlike Strasbourg, he was found guilty and given a severe sentence: five years imprisonment, 10,000 francs fine, and lifelong police surveillance (which ended, ten years later, when the Orleanist government was overthrown).

Laity's trial provided cherished publicity for Louis Napoleon. The Strasbourg coup had now been openly acknowledged by the government as a genuine threat rather than simply the theatrical act of a misled and foolhardy young man.

Chapter Nine

Epilogue

———•——

After Laity's imprisonment the French stepped up pressure on the Swiss to deport Louis Napoleon. In the midst of escalating tension, the situation was defused when the prince wrote to the president of the Lower Council of Thurgau, "I am leaving a country where my presence would serve as a pretext for such calamities as would be involved in an armed conflict," and then left Switzerland for England, arriving there on October 24, 1838.

The experience of the previous two years only reconfirmed his faith that he was destined to rule in France; and, joined by a number of veterans of Strasbourg and others, he began planning another coup to take place at Boulogne. This time there was far more careful planning and substantially more resources were committed. Instead of barely fifteen conspirators, now there were nearly sixty, including the distinguished General Count Charles de Montholon who had shared Napoleon's exile on St. Helena. Despite all this, the episode at Boulogne on August 7, 1840 was far more of a disaster than Strasbourg. Since leniency had not worked earlier, the government decided to try Louis Napoleon and a number of his co-conspirators for treason. Louis Philippe decreed that the whole peerage would judge him, but over half of the peers defied the king and did not participate, the final decree condemning Louis Napoleon to perpetual imprisonment being signed by less than half the peerage of France. His defense was not really a defense at all but a spirited defiance of the system, especially criticizing the large number of peers who, despite owing their position to the emperor, now had the temerity to judge his nephew. The result was even more publicity for Louis Napoleon. Ironically, October 7, 1840, the day Louis Napoleon entered prison at the fortress of Ham, happened also to be when the frigate *Belle Poule* arrived, returning Napoleon's body to France (the Return of the Ashes).

After remaining a prisoner for over five years and seven months, on May 25, 1846 Louis Napoleon escaped and again made his way to England. He was there when events he had nothing to do with led to the fall of Louis Philippe in February, 1848. He was likewise not associated with the appalling violence and bloodshed of the June Days, the culmination of a vicious struggle between republicans and socialists for control of the Constituent Assembly. In June by-elections for assembly seats, Persigny, Laity and others had entered Louis Napoleon's name and campaigned for him. While still in England he was elected in four departments. Sensing the impending crisis he declined the seats; but in September elections when he won in five departments, he came to Paris and was sworn in as a deputy on September 26. By November 4 the Assembly had produced a new constitution and scheduled elections. To the amazement of many seasoned politicians, on December 10, 1848, Louis Napoleon Bonaparte, the escaped convicted felon, was legitimately elected President of the Second French Republic by a landslide, his faith in the magic of his name dramatically validated.

After three years he substantially modified the structure of the Republic by means of a coup and a year later on December 2, 1852, it became history when he took the title of Napoleon III, Emperor of the French, changes all sanctioned by plebiscites. His regime, known as the Second Empire, was a period of prosperity, sumptuous imperial balls and galas, profound social and economic reform, and a foreign policy experiencing both brilliant successes and disasters. In 1870 his reign ended in the midst of the Franco-Prussian War; and nearly three years later, on January 9, 1873, he died in exile in England, at the time contemplating yet another plot to come to power in France. In 1879 his son was to perish while serving with the British Army in combat with the Zulus. While pockets of Bonapartist sympathies lingered on in France for another couple decades, with Louis Napoleon's death the Legend in action had run its course.

• • •

After the failed coup at Strasbourg those most instrumental in aiding Louis Napoleon in its planning were to reappear as factors in his life. Foremost among these was Persigny, a major figure also at Boulogne. Actively working for Louis Napoleon in the 1848 elections, he became an intimate advisor after the prince came to power, serving in a variety of appointed roles: prefect of the Loire, minister of the interior, and ambassador to both Prussia and Britain. Louis Napoleon also made him a duke, a senator, and a grand officer of the Legion of Honor. The two men had a falling out after 1863 and Persigny died in 1872.

The ever loyal Parquin was at Arenenberg in August, 1837, to greet Louis Napoleon on his return from America. He was part of the Bonaparte prince's entourage in England and instrumental in the Boulogne affair. For this he was sentenced to imprisonment for twenty years in the citadel of Doullens where he died a captive in 1845.

Among the most devoted to Louis Napoleon after Strasbourg was Vaudrey. He was at Arenenberg in December of 1837 and in his London retinue in 1838. Prominent at Boulogne he was one of the intimate few the new president invited to an inauguration day dinner at the Elysée Palace on December 20, 1848. Further honors bestowed upon him included promotion to brigadier general, appointment as aide-de-camp to the president, Commander of the Legion of Honor, and Governor of the Hotel des Invalides, Napoleon's final resting place.

Numbering with Persigny, Parquin, and Vaudrey among the most dedicated was Laity. The Boulogne incident occurred while he was imprisoned; but upon his release in 1843, he visited Louis

Napoleon at Ham. In 1848 he was briefly imprisoned (the third time) for his tireless work in promoting Louis Napoleon's candidacy in by-elections for seats in the Assembly. Active also in the presidential campaign, Laity was at the inauguration day celebration dinner on December 20. In February, 1849, President Louis Napoleon named him a Chevalier in the Legion of Honor, the first in many honors over the next twenty years. The final mark of distinction came in 1869 when Captain Laity was listed as a regency council member should Prince Napoleon (Jerome's son) come to power, presuming the prior deaths of Napoleon III and the Empress Eugenie.

Among the more devoted veterans of Strasbourg, Querelles was at Arenenberg welcoming Louis on his return from America. He was at Boulogne but never captured and tried in absentia. Although he died in 1847, his sister worked closely with Persigny in Louis Napoleon's behalf in 1848. Both she and Querelles' son were to receive pensions during the Second Empire.

Also at Boulogne and sentenced to twenty years was Lombard. After his early release gossip circulated that he had sold information to Adolphe Thiers; and although he was given 20,000 francs in 1853, he played no important role in the Second Empire.

Another dedicated supporter to be at Arenenberg when Louis Napoleon returned from America was Gricourt. His devotion was rewarded handsomely during the Second Empire when he became successively chamberlain, senator, and finally in 1870 one of only nine commanders in the Legion of Honor. Of the veterans of the Strasbourg coup, he received the largest remuneration by far, 42,000 francs per year for nineteen years (798,000 francs) in addition to other indemnities, for a grand recorded total of 1,011,000 francs.

After Strasbourg Eleonore Gordon received occasional visits from Vaudrey, but the affair was clearly over. In 1839 she visited Louis Napoleon in England and later visited him at Ham. With Madame Salvage she settled in Paris where she was watched like a hawk by the police. In 1848 she worked in Louis Napoleon's election campaigns; and when he became president, she expected far more recognition than a modest 4800 franc pension. When she indignantly complained at the Elysée, she was given 5000 francs and curtly dismissed. Disappointed and disillusioned, she passed away shortly thereafter, her funeral expenses (720 francs) being paid by Louis Napoleon.

The last of the major conspirators at Strasbourg was de Bruc, the least supportive and aggressive defending the coup at the trial. His family threatened to disinherit him because of his association with Louis Napoleon; and in early 1853 he approached the new emperor, reminded him of his "devotion," and asked for an appointment as "commandant de chateau" or some such appropriate position. He also had the temerity to request fifteen years army back pay, from 1838 to 1853, at 2000 francs per year, but settled for less than half the amount when Napoleon III, doubtless with mixed emotions, paid him 12,000 francs. This was only a prelude however to continued financial demands.

Another principal from his early life surfaced in the form of Valerie Masuyer. Among the host of rumors circulating earlier about the coup were some that questioned whether or not Valerie had betrayed the plotters, and at some time Louis Napoleon may have believed this. In his letters to Hortense from America he included greetings to Madame Salvage but nothing personal to Valerie. When he returned to Arenenberg, he deliberately shunned her. After Hortense died, Louis Napoleon learned from Valerie that he had a half-brother, Auguste de Morny, the son of his mother and Flahaut. This information struck him like a thunderbolt. He had not the faintest inclination of this indiscretion of his mother and adjusted uneasily to the news. During the Second Empire Morny was hated by Persigny but played a role of some prominence as Louis designated him the President of the Legislative Body and also made him a duke. In order that she might tend the tomb of Hortense, Valerie settled not far from Malmaision near Rueil where

Hortense and her mother Josephine were buried. This sufficiently moved Louis Napoleon that after the Second Empire was proclaimed, he gave her a suite in the Tuileries.

A Note On Sources

The Orleanist-republican version of Louis Napoleon's Strasbourg coup has now endured for over 160 years. Over that period another bit of folklore has also developed, the idea that the real truth of the coup cannot be ascertained because when Louis Napoleon finally came to power, pertinent government records were removed from the archives and destroyed or had disappeared. This assertion stems from an incident which occurred less than three weeks after Louis Napoleon's election as President of the Second French Republic. On December 27, 1848, he rather brusquely and imperiously instructed the minister of the interior, Léon de Maleville, to have delivered to him by the next Thursday sixteen cartons of dossiers on the affairs of Strasbourg and Boulogne. This correspondence had an electric effect. De Maleville regarded the letter as insolent and immediately submitted his resignation to the head of the ministry, who then happened to be Odilon Barrot. Barrot at once convened his colleagues who unanimously joined de Maleville in submitting their resignations. Among the group were Léon Faucher, de Falloux, and Drouyn de Lhuys. Taken aback, Louis Napoleon expressed surprise at any hint his request was inappropriate or offensive to the minister of the interior and wrote a letter profusely apologizing and urging them not to resign. De Maleville alone persisted in resigning and the incident was over. If materials were subsequently delivered to Louis Napoleon, the most likely time would have been between the coup of December 2, 1851, when his power was enhanced enormously, and October of 1852. In November, 1852, a fairly thorough 26 page inventory was prepared, perhaps in apprehension of a future request which would then come from an emperor in the Tuileries rather than a president in the Elysée. The inventory is still accurate, but some earlier tampering with dossiers clearly seems to have occurred. Nonetheless, substantial amounts of archival material have survived relating to the Strasbourg incident. At the Archives Nationales in the F[1c] series on public morale, reports of the prefects of the Lower Rhine are missing for the reign of Louis Philippe. Similarly, in BB[18] and BB[30] on political events, most of the political reports of the procureur generals are missing for 1830 – 1850. On the other hand, nos. 767 and 768 in the CC (Chamber of Peers) series of documents on the struggle against political societies contain extensive materials on Louis Napoleon's coup. CC 767 has folders of the pretrial testimony taken from all the principals in the trial and from others involved in any way, such as innkeepers or incidental witnesses to events. There is a document signed by Talandier, which clarifies how he spelled his name which appears in official, semi-official and secondary sources spelled in a variety of ways. There are other materials, including some pamphlets and also, quite out of place, a report to the procureur general at Colmar, dated 1838, pertaining to Laity's trial. CC 768 contains a variety of correspondence involving the conspirators as well as some address and account books. There are also separate folios on de Bruc, Persigny, and Vaudrey.

At the Archives Historique of the Ministry of War the ministry correspondence with generals commanding the military districts from 1830 to 1848 comprises a valuable resource of 138 cartons. As well as dealing with military events, there is also considerable information on the political atmosphere which supplements the reports of civil authorities. In the ministry's Archives Administratives are a host of reports of general officers and their subordinates which are indispensable sources for understanding events in Alsace under Louis Philippe.

There are a variety of other repositories with material relating to the coup, including municipal archives in the Strasbourg area, the Strasbourg City Archive, and especially the Department of Manuscripts in the Strasbourg City Library. Mention should also be made of a special folio of 38 letters (14 to Hortense) written by Louis Napoleon between March 24, 1836, and July 2, 1838. These are at Arenenberg, now a museum, as part of its small library dealing almost exclusively with works relating to the life of Louis Napoleon. Duplicates of several of the letters, including Louis Napoleon's own account of the failed coup, are part of the manuscript holdings of Dartmouth College. For the best guide to repositories of unpublished documents, see pages xxv – xxxiv in the bibliography of Félix Ponteil's *L'opposition politique a Strasbourg sous la monarchie de juillet (1830-1848)*. Paris, 1932. Our study and these comments profit substantially from Ponteil's impressive bibliography and his examination of both the social context in which the coup occurred and the coup itself. While the coup and the trial were reported in the *Moniteur*, relevant coup documents and the verbatim court proceedings are conveniently available in Albert Fermé, S*trasbourg d'après les documents authentiques*. Paris, 1868.

A host of memoirs and contemporary accounts are of special interest, including: Louis Blanc, *The History of Ten Years. 1830 – 1840*, vol. 2. 2 vols., London, 1895; Odilon Barrot, *Mémoires posthumes de Odilon Barrot*, vol. 1. 4 vols., Paris, 1875-76; Alexandre Dumas, *The Last King*, vol. 2. 2 vols., N.Y. 1915 (first published in Paris 1852); François Guizot, *Mémoires pour server a l'histoire de mon temps*, vols. 2, 3. 8 vols., Paris, 1858-67; and Valérie Masuyer, *Mémoires, lettres et papiers de Valérie Masuyer*. Paris, 1937. One memoir merits a special note of caution, that of Baron d'Ambès, *Intimate Memoirs of Napoleon III: Personal Reminiscences of the Man and the Emperor*. 2 vols., London, 1910. D'Ambès was a pseudonym for George-Charles d'Anthès, Baron Heeckeren. At St. Petersburg in 1837 he had killed Pushkin in a duel. An early supporter of Louis Napoleon and a senator during the Second

Empire, his memoirs were compiled in 1893 from scattered notes and recollections which some scholars have regarded as unreliable. He claimed an intimate friendship with Louis Napoleon beginning in 1833. A regular at Arenenberg, he described himself as being present at much of the coup's planning and playing an active role during the coup. On the face of it, his detailed narrative seems convincing; but despite this, he is not mentioned even once in the major records relating to the coup. Accordingly, in our account we have not mentioned him nor relied on him for any information which rests only on his testimony.

Important correspondence regarding the coup may also be found in the first two volumes of Blanchard Jerrold, *The Life of Napoleon III*. 4 vols., London, 1874-1882. This "authorized" biography was biased but blessed with access to a substantial number of family records. His account of the coup contains some inaccuracies but generally follows Laity's account. In the twentieth century, the hostile republican version of Louis Napoleon was joined by a more favorable revisionist perspective, largely started by F.A. Simpson's *The Rise of Louis Napoleon*. London, 1909. In this, the story of the coup generally follows Laity and Jerrold. Simpson includes some correspondence but not nearly as much or as complete as what Jerrold provides.

Of special interest regarding the coup are the following: H. Thirria, *Napoléon III avant l'Empire*. Paris, 1895; André Lebey, *Les Trois Coups D'Etat de Louis-Napoléon Bonaparte* (vol. 1, Strasbourg et Boulogne). 2 vols., Paris, 1906; and volume nine of Jean B.H.R. Capefigue, *L'Europe depuis l'avénement du roi Louis-Philippe*, 10 vols., Paris, 1846.

Index